CAMBRIDGE
UNIVERSITY PRESS

CAMBRIDGE
Primary English

Learner's Book 3

Sarah Lindsay & Kate Ruttle

CAMBRIDGE
UNIVERSITY PRESS

University Printing House, Cambridge CB2 8BS, United Kingdom

One Liberty Plaza, 20th Floor, New York, NY 10006, USA

477 Williamstown Road, Port Melbourne, VIC 3207, Australia

314–321, 3rd Floor, Plot 3, Splendor Forum, Jasola District Centre,
New Delhi – 110025, India

103 Penang Road, #05–06/07, Visioncrest Commercial, Singapore 238467

Cambridge University Press is part of the University of Cambridge.

It furthers the University's mission by disseminating knowledge in the pursuit of
education, learning and research at the highest international levels of excellence.

www.cambridge.org
Information on this title: www.cambridge.org/9781108819541

First published 2015
Second edition 2021

20 19 18 17 16 15 14 13 12 11 10 9 8 7 6 5 4 3 2 1

Printed in Malaysia by Vivar Printing

A catalogue record for this publication is available from the British Library

ISBN 978-1-108-81954-1 Paperback with Digital Access (1 Year)
ISBN 978-1-108-96422-7 Digital Learner's Book (1 Year)
ISBN 978-1-108-96414-2 eBook

Additional resources for this publication at www.cambridge.org/go

Cambridge University Press has no responsibility for the persistence or accuracy
of URLs for external or third-party internet websites referred to in this publication,
and does not guarantee that any content on such websites is, or will remain,
accurate or appropriate. Information regarding prices, travel timetables, and other
factual information given in this work is correct at the time of first printing but
Cambridge University Press does not guarantee the accuracy of such information
thereafter.

....

Introduction

Welcome to Stage 3 of Cambridge Primary English.

In this book you'll read exciting adventure stories, myths, legends and playscripts. You will plan a party, learn about letters and discover more about countries. We've found you poems from around the world and funny riddles and jokes that play with words. In all the units, there are texts for you to read, enjoy and talk about, as well as the chance to use your ideas to write your own versions.

English can be great fun as you learn to get better at:

- sharing your thoughts and ideas with your partners
- improving your vocabulary
- working with others as you discuss, act, play, and make
- reading and sharing new stories, poems and ideas
- writing down your ideas.

It's always useful to share your ideas with partners. When you share ideas, your partner can often help you to improve them. And you can help your partner too. Throughout the units, you will be asked to think about what you have done or learnt. You will also be asked to discuss how you learnt so that you can become an even better learner. At the end of each unit, there are ideas for projects we hope you will enjoy. They will help you to build on what you have learnt. We hope you will enjoy reading and exploring the stories, playscripts, letters, poems and information texts in this book.

Sarah Lindsay & Kate Ruttle

Contents

...eaking/Listening	Language focus	Cross-curricular links	21st century skills
...ad a setting description to a partner ...an interesting way ...ten to a character description ...lk about what happens next in a ...ory in a group ...t out *The Enormous Crocodile*	Nouns and adjectives Verbs Speech marks Writing dialogue	Science: Plants; shadows; describing material properties; sorting and classifying Maths: Size vocabulary; writing numbers as words; comparing measurements History: Chronological study Art: Colour mixing IT: Writing simple code for an animation	Use critical thinking to work out the meaning of new vocabulary Work collaboratively in a group to predict what happens next in a story
...lk about celebrations ...an a class party in a group ...sten to a conversation about a party ...ve spoken instructions	Command verbs and sequencing words in instructional texts Adding -ing or -ed to words	Science: Reading and writing instructions in experiments; listing planets alphabetically Maths: Exploring measurement; direction and turning about a point; money	Communicate experiences of a celebration Work collaboratively to plan a class party
...erform a poem to others ...scuss the features of a poem ...sten to a news report ...erform a favourite poem	Rules for verb endings Noun phrases Onomatopoeia Syllables	Science: Identifying parts of a plant; investigating sound; drawing tables to record results Maths: Symmetry in plants; lengths of rivers; syllables in shape words Geography: Weather around the world; Rainforests Art: Japanese art	Work creatively to write a new verse for a poem Communicate ideas for how to improve a poetry performance
...scuss likes and dislikes ...erform a story in a group ...iscuss similarities and differences ...etween myths and legends ...sten to a myth ...ole play characters from a myth ...ell a story to a partner	Pronouns Suffixes Paragraphs Multi-clause sentences and connectives Contractions Dialogue	Science: Investigating shadows; how scientific ideas have changed; features of animals History: Tribes of North America; exploring heroes and legends from own culture; trade routes of the Indian Ocean	Communicate opinions of a story to others Reflect on strategies for remembering spellings
...lk about differences between ...canning and reading carefully ...iscuss when to use formal and ...formal letters ...sten to a conversation between ...unty Sonia and Arturo ...lk about receiving mail ...ell the story of Mrs Sabella's trip	Prepositions Synonyms Parts of a letter Homophones Punctuation	Maths: 24-hour clock; calculating time intervals; Days, weeks, months, years History: Family trees Geography: Famous landmarks; researching rivers; transport of mail	Collaborate with a partner to write synonyms for happy and sad Communicate experiences of receiving mail

Contents

How to use this book

In this book you will find lots of different features to help your learning.

What you will learn in the unit. →

> **We are going to...**
> - read and answer questions about a poem from Bahamas.

Questions to find out what you know already. →

> **Getting started**
> 1 Do you know the story *Charlie and the Chocolate Factory* by Roald Dahl?
>   It is about a boy, Charlie Bucket, who won a golden ticket to meet Mr Wonka and visit his amazing chocolate factory.
> 2 Talk about how you think Charlie felt before meeting Mr Wonka and visiting the factory.
> 3 Would you like to visit a chocolate factory? Why?

Fun activities linked to what you are learning. →

> 1 When you read a poem, do you always know which country it is from?
>   a Talk about the clues you might find in a poem to tell you which country the poem was written in. If a poem was from your town, region or country, what would it say?

Important words to learn. →

> **Key word**
>
> definition: the meaning of a word

Audio recordings of texts and listening activities. →

Key language and grammar rules explained. →

> **Language focus**
>
> Nouns are words we use to name things.
> **Examples:** house, bed, shop, beach, hill, flower
> Adjectives are words we use to describe nouns.
> **Examples:** big, small, pretty, lovely, nice, dirty, horrible, high, low

Questions to help you think about how you learn.

> How can you remember to use interesting dialogue words in your own writing?

Hints to help you with your reading, writing, speaking and listening skills.

Listening tip

Make sure everyone in the group listens to each other.

A good time to pause and find out how your learning is progressing.

How are we doing?

Ask your partner to check your piles of books. They can draw you a smiley face if you have got the books all in the right piles, or a sad face if you need to change some.

This is what you have learned in the unit.

Look what I can do!

- ☐ I can read and answer questions about poems.
- ☐ I can read aloud with expression.
- ☐ I can write a poem that includes powerful words and noun phrases.
- ☐ I can recognise onomatopoeic words and include some in my own writing.
- ☐ I can write a haiku.
- ☐ I can compare and review poems.

Questions that cover what you have learned in the unit. If you can answer these, you are ready to move on to the next unit.

Check your progress

1 In this unit you have read instructions for making:
   - a cake
   - a pop-up card
   - some fruit rockets.
   Write a list of all the things that are the same about these instructions.
2 What other non-fiction texts are in this unit?
3 Write two sentences, each starting with a command verb.

Projects for you to carry out, using what you have learned. You might make something or solve a problem.

Projects

Group project: Write your own recipe for something you love to eat. It could be something you create yourself. As a group, discuss how you are going to display your recipes to create a recipe book.

Pair project: Imagine you and a partner are running the class party. Write a list of everything that needs to be done on the day. Then write the things on your list in the order they need to be done, starting with what you need to do first.

1 > Story writing with Roald Dahl

> 1.1 Setting the scene

We are going to...

- explore and write about different story settings.

Getting started

1 Look at these photographs. They each show a setting.

2 In a group, talk about the places you can see.

3 Collect words to describe one of the settings. Share the words you have collected.

1 Answer these questions.

a Have you visited any places similar to the settings in the photographs?

b Why were you there?

c What did you do there?

d Did you enjoy being there?

e Did anything interesting happen while you were there?

Key word

setting: a place where something can happen, for example an event, or a story

> All the photos could be settings for a story. Stories often begin with a setting so the reader can imagine where the story begins.

2 We use **nouns** and **adjectives** when we write story settings.

Language focus

Nouns are words we use to name things.

Examples: house, bed, shop, beach, hill, flower

Adjectives are words we use to describe nouns.

Examples: big, small, pretty, lovely, nice, dirty, horrible, high, low

a Talk about nouns and adjectives you could use when you describe each of the photographs.

b In your notebook, write four sentences, one for each photograph. Use at least one noun and one adjective in each sentence.

3 Choose one of the photos.

   a   Read the sentences you wrote about it aloud.

   b   Talk about a story that could happen in this setting.

> ## 1.2 Looking at a setting

We are going to...

- **read and answer questions about a setting.**

Getting started

1   Have you heard of the author Roald Dahl? He wrote all his books in a shed in his back garden! He was an amazing storyteller because his words build pictures in our minds.

2   Find out some other facts about Roald Dahl. Can you list any books he wrote?

1   This is an extract from *Matilda* by Roald Dahl.

Matilda is a very special young girl.
Only Miss Honey, her teacher, understands how special she is.

Read the description of Miss Honey's home.

Miss Honey's Home

Matilda saw a narrow dirt-path leading to a tiny red-brick cottage. The cottage was so small it looked more like a doll's house than a **human dwelling**. The bricks it was built of were old and crumbly and very pale red. It had a slate roof and one small chimney, and there were two little windows at the front. Each window was no larger than a sheet of newspaper and there was clearly no upstairs to the place. On either side of the path there was a **wilderness** of nettles and thorns and long brown grass. An enormous oak tree stood overshadowing the cottage. Its massive spreading branches seemed to be **embracing** the tiny building, and perhaps hiding it as well from the rest of the world.

Roald Dahl

Glossary

human dwelling: a place where people live

wilderness: a wild area

embracing: holding something closely

Reading tip

If you don't know what a word means:

- think of other words that look and sound similar, for example *wonderful* looks like *wonder* with the suffix *–ful* added
- read the rest of the sentence and see if you can work it out
- look up the word in a dictionary.

2 Answer these questions in your notebook.

    a Who lives in the house Matilda is visiting?

    b Does the house have a chimney?

    c Does the house have an upstairs?

    d Do you think the house is described well?

    e Would you like to live in this house? Why?

3 Think about the nouns and adjectives Roald Dahl uses.

    a List three nouns Roald Dahl uses in the setting of Miss Honey's house.

    b List three adjectives Roald Dahl uses in the setting of Miss Honey's house.

How do you find the nouns and adjectives in a text?
Do you find it easier to find the nouns or the adjectives?

> 1.3 Building a picture with words

We are going to...

- **discuss the different sounds the letters ou make in words.**

Getting started

1 Do you know the story *Danny the Champion of the World* by Roald Dahl?

   It is about a boy, Danny, whose mother died when he was a baby. Danny lives in a caravan in the countryside with his father.

2 Talk about how Danny might have felt growing up with his father.

3 What do you think he might have enjoyed?

4 What do you think he might have missed?

1   Read the description of Danny and his father's home to yourself.

The caravan

The caravan was our house and our home. It was a real old **gipsy wagon** with big wheels and fine patterns painted all over it in yellow and red and blue. My father said it was at least a hundred and fifty years old.

There was only one room in the caravan and it wasn't much bigger than a fair-sized modern bathroom. It was a narrow room, the shape of the caravan itself, and against the back wall were two **bunk beds**, one above the other. The top one was my father's, the bottom one mine.

There was a wood-burning stove with a chimney that went through the roof, and this kept us warm in winter.

For furniture, we had two chairs and a small table, and those, apart from a tiny chest of drawers, were all the home comforts we **possessed**. They were all we needed.

I really loved living in that **gipsy caravan**. I loved it especially in the evenings when I was tucked up in my bunk and my father was telling me stories. The **paraffin lamp** was turned low, and I could see lumps of wood glowing red-hot in the old stove and wonderful it was to be lying there snug and warm in my bunk in that little room. Most wonderful of all was the feeling that when I went to sleep, my father would still be there, very close to me, sitting in his chair by the fire, or lying in the bunk above my own.

Roald Dahl

Glossary

gipsy wagon / caravan: a traditional horse-drawn home for people who travel from place to place

bunk beds: one bed above another bed

possessed: owned

paraffin lamp: a lamp that has a flame lit with paraffin

15 >

Re-read the setting description aloud to a partner.
Read it in an interesting way so that your partner wants
to keep listening.

Speaking tip

If you are stuck on how to read a word, try to:

- sound it out (look at the whole word for a spelling pattern you know, for example, the words *stove* and *close* have o_e so usually the o sound is long)

- divide it into syllables (*narrow* can be split into two syllables: *nar-row*)

- match it to other words you know (*bigger* is from the word family *big*)

Key word

syllable: a single sound in a spoken word that helps to give it rhythm

2   Answer the questions.

   a   What colour is Danny's caravan painted?

   b   Is Danny's caravan new?

   c   How many rooms does the caravan have?

   d   What keeps Danny and his father warm in winter?

   e   List the items of furniture Danny and his father have.

   f   Would you like to live in Danny's caravan?

3   Look at the ou words in the text.

   a   Read these ou words aloud.

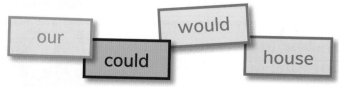

   b   How many different ways do you pronounce the ou sound?

   c   List the words that have the same ou sound.

4 You are now going to draw a picture.

  a Read the extract together again.
    Think about the picture that it is making in your mind.

  b Draw a picture of Danny's caravan.
    You can either draw the outside or the inside.

  c Compare your drawing with a partner's drawing.
    What things look the same?

  d Do you think Roald Dahl managed to make a clear picture
    of Danny's caravan using words?

〉 1.4 Writing a setting

We are going to...

- **write sentences describing settings.**

Getting started

1 With a partner, talk about some places you know well.

2 Talk about different nouns and adjectives you would use
  if you wrote about a setting you know well.

1   Look at these settings. They are the same place but at different times.

a   Talk about what is the same and what is different in the two pictures.

A setting can include information about:
• the weather (... in a noisy thunderstorm)
• the time (First thing in the morning ...).

b Look at these adjectives in the boxes.
Copy the table into your notebook.
Add the adjectives that describe each picture to the table.

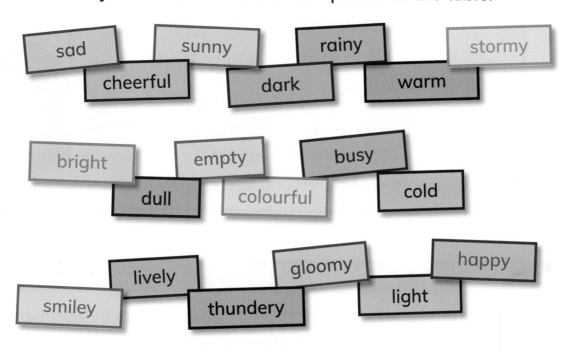

Picture 1	Picture 2
sunny	

c Write three sentences to describe the setting for each of the pictures.
The sentences can describe the place, the weather or the time.

Remember that adjectives
can go before or after the noun.
Examples: It was a narrow room.

adjective   noun

The room was narrow.

noun   adjective

2   Write three sentences about a setting you know well.
Think carefully about which adjectives you use to describe
your setting.

How are we doing?

Read your sentences to a partner. Do they think you have described
the setting well? Can they suggest other adjectives you might use?

> 1.5 | Looking at characters

We are going to...

- **read and write about story characters.**

Getting started

1   Do you know the story *Charlie and the Chocolate Factory* by Roald Dahl?

It is about a boy, Charlie Bucket, who won a golden ticket to meet
Mr Wonka and visit his amazing chocolate factory.

2   Talk about how you think Charlie felt before meeting Mr Wonka and
visiting the factory.

3   Would you like to visit a chocolate factory? Why?

1 When we meet characters in a story, we usually want to know the following four things about them:

- what they look like
- what they do
- what they think or say
- how they feel.

Read this description of Mr Wonka from *Charlie and the Chocolate Factory* by Roald Dahl.

Writing about a character is like writing about a setting. The words describe the character so you can build a picture of that person in your mind.

Mr Wonka

Mr Wonka was standing all alone just inside the open gates of the factory.

And what an **extraordinary** little man he was!

He had a black top hat on his head.

He wore a tail coat made of beautiful plum-coloured velvet.

His trousers were bottle green.

His gloves were pearly grey.

And in one hand he carried a fine gold-topped walking cane.

Covering his chin, there was a small, neat, pointed black beard – a goatee. And his eyes – his eyes were **marvellously** bright. They seemed to be sparkling and twinkling at you all the time. The whole face, in fact, was **alight** with fun and laughter.

And oh, how clever he looked! How quick and sharp and full of life! He kept making quick **jerky** little movements with his head, cocking it this way and that, and taking everything in with those bright twinkling eyes.

Roald Dahl

Glossary

extraordinary: very special

marvellously: wonderfully

alight: showing clearly

jerky: sudden and quick

Did you know that when Roald Dahl was at boarding school, he was invited to try out new chocolate bars. This inspired him to write the story *Charlie and the Chocolate Factory!*

In a group, discuss this description of Mr Wonka.

a   What does he look like?

b   What does he do?

c   What might he be thinking?

d   How does he feel?

The text might not tell us about all these things.

 2   Listen to this description of Charlie while he is waiting in line to enter Mr Wonka's chocolate factory.

a   List as many adjectives as you can that describe Charlie.

Listening tip

Make sure everyone in the group listens to each other.

b   Write your own character description of Charlie.

c   Share your character description with your group.

> 1.6 What happens next?

We are going to...

- **explore setting and character descriptions in the text.**

Getting started

In a group, talk about these questions.

1   What do you know about crocodiles?

2   Do you know where crocodiles live?

3   Do you know what crocodiles eat?

1   Read the start of *The Enormous Crocodile* by Roald Dahl.

The Enormous Crocodile

In the biggest, brownest muddiest river in Africa, two crocodiles lay with their heads just above the water. One of the crocodiles was enormous. The other was not so big.

'Do you know what I would like for my lunch today?' the Enormous Crocodile asked.

'No,' the Notsobig One said. 'What?'

The Enormous Crocodile grinned, showing hundreds of sharp white teeth. 'For my lunch today,' he said, 'I would like a nice juicy little child.'

'I never eat children,' the Notsobig One said. 'Only fish.'

'Ho, ho, ho!' cried the Enormous Crocodile. 'I'll bet if you saw a fat juicy little child paddling in the water over there at this very moment, you'd gulp him up in one gollop!'

'No, I wouldn't,' the Notsobig One said. 'Children are too tough and chewy. They are tough and chewy and nasty and bitter.'

'*Tough* and *chewy*!' cried the Enormous Crocodile. '*Nasty* and *bitter*! What awful tommy-rot you talk! They are juicy and yummy!'

'They taste so bitter,' the Notsobig One said, 'you have to cover them with sugar before you can eat them.'

'Children are bigger than fish,' said the Enormous Crocodile. 'You get bigger helpings.'

'You are greedy,' the Notsobig One said. 'You're the greediest croc in the whole river.'

'I'm the bravest croc in the whole river,' said the Enormous Crocodile. 'I'm the only one who dares to leave the water and go through the jungle to the town to look for little children to eat.'

'You've only done that once,' snorted the Notsobig One. 'And what happened then? They all saw you coming and ran away.'

'Ah, but today when I go, they won't see me at all,' said the Enormous Crocodile.

'Of course they'll see you,' the Notsobig One said. 'You're so enormous and ugly, they'll see you from miles away.'

The Enormous Crocodile grinned again, and his terrible sharp teeth sparkled like knives in the sun. 'Nobody will see me,' he said, 'because this time I've thought up secret plans and clever tricks.'

Roald Dahl

2 Talk about the answers to these questions.

   a   Where is this story set?

   b   What adjectives are used to describe the setting?

   c   Who are the main characters?

   d   Describe the characters.

   e   What is clever about the Notsobig One's name?

What do you think the word *enormous* means? There is a clue in the first few sentences.

3 Write answers to these questions in your notebook.

   a   What does the Enormous Crocodile want for his lunch?

   b   What does the Notsobig One eat?

   c   Why doesn't the Notsobig One like to eat children?

   d   Why does the Enormous Crocodile think he is the bravest crocodile in the river?

   e   Do you think the two crocodiles like each other? Why?

   f   What do you think the Enormous Crocodile's secret plans and clever tricks might be?

4 In a group, talk about what you think happens next in the story.

> 1.7 Looking at verbs

We are going to...

- look at verbs in the past and present tense.

Getting started

1 Do you remember what a verb is?

2 Give an example of a verb.

3 How do we know it is a verb?

Language focus

Verbs tell you what someone or something *does*, *is* or *has*. Verbs are sometimes called *doing words*, but they are also *being* or *having words*.

Verbs also tell you when the action in the sentence happens.

Examples:

What?	When?	Tense
He **walked** to school.	Has already happened	past
She **walks** to school.	Is happening now	present

The verb *to be* is the most common verb in the English language. Different parts of the verb are tricky to recognise. They include the little words *am*, *is*, *are*, *was* and *were*.

1 Which of these are sentences? Copy the sentences.
<u>Underline</u> the verb in each sentence.

   a The big crocodile.

   b He swims towards the river bank.

   c I love fish.

   d He hears some children.

   e Some dangerous crocodiles.

   f They eat their lunch together.

> **Writing tip**
>
> A sentence must:
>
> - have a verb (if there isn't a verb, it isn't a sentence)
> - begin with a capital letter
> - end with a full stop, question mark or exclamation mark
> - make sense.

2   Write these sentences in your notebook.
    Add the correct form of the verb to be (am, is, are, was or were).

   a   When he _____ two, the Enormous Crocodile
       liked eating fish.

   b   He _____ very good at catching fish.

   c   Now he _____ bigger he likes to eat children.

   d   'I _____ very hungry,' said the Enormous Crocodile.

3   Write whether each of these sentences is in the past or the
    present tense.

   a   The Enormous Crocodile smiled at the Notsobig One.

   b   The Notsobig One eats her fish quickly.

   c   The Enormous Crocodile crawled out of the water.

   d   The Notsobig One laughed at the Enormous Crocodile.

   e   The Enormous Crocodile walks off
       into the jungle.

27

> 1.8 Speech in texts

We are going to...

- use speech marks to show dialogue and explore different verbs to describe speech in texts.

Getting started

1 Look at this cartoon. What do you think the children are saying?

2 Discuss how we know when someone is speaking in a story.

3 Find some examples of someone speaking in a book you are reading.

1 Look carefully at the story *The Enormous Crocodile* by Roald Dahl in Session 1.6. Answer the questions.

 a How do we know what the characters say to each other in the story?

 b How many characters are talking in this part of the story?

 c Who are they?

 d How do we know when the Enormous Crocodile is talking?

Language focus

Speech marks are placed around the words that are said by a character.

Example: *'Is it lunch time?' asked the Enormous Crocodile.*

2 Copy these sentences. Add the missing speech marks to the dialogue.

   a Shall we walk to the river? asked Anja.

   b Yes, good idea! said Juan.

   c We will have to be careful, explained Anja.

   d Why? asked Juan.

   e There may be crocodiles, laughed Anja.

3 Re-read the whole story.

> **Key word**
>
> dialogue:
> talking between
> characters in
> a story

Language focus

When you write dialogue, you use a verb to show how a character is feeling when they speak.

The verbs can come before or after the dialogue.

Example: *She screamed, 'Watch out!'*
           'Watch out!' she screamed.

We start a new line each time a different character says something.

---

   a List the verbs used to describe how the dialogue is said.
      Which verbs are used instead of *said*?

   b When the word *said* is used, think of a different verb Roald Dahl
      could have used instead.

   c Read the sentences in the boxes aloud with expression to a partner.
      Use the verb to work out how to say the words. Talk about how and
      why you changed the way you said the words.

   'Good morning,' he said.   'Good morning,' she sobbed.

   'Good morning,' she mumbled.   'Good morning,' he whispered.

   'Good morning,' he yelled.

4   Copy these sentences. Add the missing speech marks.
    Add a verb to describe how the dialogue is said.
    Use a different verb in each sentence.

   a   Is that a crocodile over there?
       _____ Anja.

   b   Juan _____ Where?

   c   Over there, near the tree in the
       water, _____ Anja.

   d   Oh yes! I can see it,
       _____ Juan.

   e   Anja _____, Quick,
       let's run!

How can you remember to use interesting dialogue words
in your own writing?

> ## 1.9 Sequencing events

We are going to...

- **discuss the structure of stories.**

Getting started

1   Re-read the beginning of *The Enormous Crocodile* in Session 1.6.

2   In a group, discuss what you think might happen next.

1   The following sentences tell us how *The Enormous Crocodile* story
    starts and how it continues.

a Look at the sentences and, in a group, discuss the main events in the story.

b Decide the order in which these events happen.

i The Enormous Crocodile leaves the river saying he has secret plans and clever tricks to catch a child to eat.

ii The Enormous Crocodile tries out his secret plans and clever tricks.

iii The elephant grabs the Enormous Crocodile by the tail and swings him round and round. When he lets go, the Enormous Crocodile flies into space and is never seen again.

iv The Enormous Crocodile tells the Notsobig One he is going to eat a little child for lunch.

v The jungle animals help protect the children. They warn the children that the Enormous Crocodile is trying to catch them.

vi The Enormous Crocodile meets other jungle animals. He tells them about his plan to eat a child. None of them like his idea. They all like the children in the town.

How did you decide the correct order of these events?
Were there clues or words in the sentences that helped you?

2 Look at the story mountain.

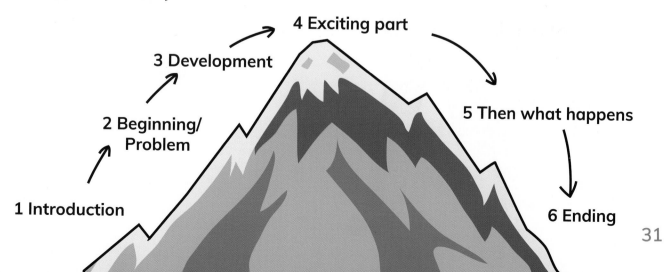

4 Exciting part

3 Development

5 Then what happens

2 Beginning/ Problem

1 Introduction

6 Ending

a Use the six main events in Activity 1 to make a story mountain.

b Talk about where each event should go.

c Copy and label the diagram with the events.

3 Act the story.

a Decide who will play the different characters in the story.

b Act a version of the story using your story mountain.

Writing tip

The story mountain shows the shape of most stories. You can use it to plan your own stories or to understand the events in a story you have read.

How are we doing?

In a group, talk about how you could improve your play if you acted your version of the story again.

> 1.10 Planning a story

We are going to...

- **plan a story.**

Getting started

1 Name all the different characters you have met in the Roald Dahl stories in this unit.

2 Talk about the character you like the best.
  Explain why you like this character.

3 Write down three adjectives that you would use to describe this character.

1 Think of an idea for a new story.

a Discuss ideas for a new story based on a character from a Roald Dahl book. Choose one of your ideas in Getting started to write about.

b Draw a story mountain in your notebook and plot the main events of your story.

If you don't have any ideas for a story, you could use one of these:

- Matilda wants to be in the school football team but her headteacher says she is too small.

- Charlie gets lost in Mr Wonka's chocolate factory.

- Danny is given a pony to tow his caravan.
  He moves to a new place where strange things happen.

2 Think about the setting and characters in your story.

a Write some notes about them at the side of your story mountain.

b Your story mountain and notes will be your plan.

3 Tell your story to yourself. Remember to include some dialogue.

   a   Now tell your story to a partner.

   b   Change your story plan to include any new ideas that you or your partner had about your story.

How are we doing?

Ask your partner what you could do to make your story better.

> 1.11 Writing a story

We are going to...

- write a story.

Getting started

Retell your story from Session 1.10 to a partner.
This will help you when you write your story.

1 Before you start writing, build a bank of adjectives and verbs.

   a   Write three adjectives about the setting in your story.

   b   Write three adjectives about each character in your story.

   c   Write three dialogue verbs you might use in your story.

2 Write your story. Follow your story mountain plan. Remember to include:

- a setting
- a description of the character or characters
- some dialogue.

How am I doing?

Read through your story.

Have you included a setting, character descriptions and some dialogue?

> 1.12 Improving your story

We are going to...

- improve the story we have written and check it for errors.

Getting started

1 Re-read the story you wrote in Session 1.11.

2 Have you followed your plan?

3 Have you included everything from your plan?

1 Think about how you can improve the story you have written.

a Could your descriptions be better?
Could you add other adjectives which make the descriptions of your setting and characters clearer?

b Have you added enough dialogue so that your story flows?

c Is the ending interesting? Does it end the story well?

Good handwriting helps your reader to enjoy your story. Is your handwriting a good size, with regular spaces between the letters and between the words?

2 **Proofread** your final story.

Re-read your story and check it carefully for any mistakes.
Check:

- the grammar
- the spelling
- the punctuation.

It is always a good
idea to proofread your
writing, just in case you
have made any small
mistakes.

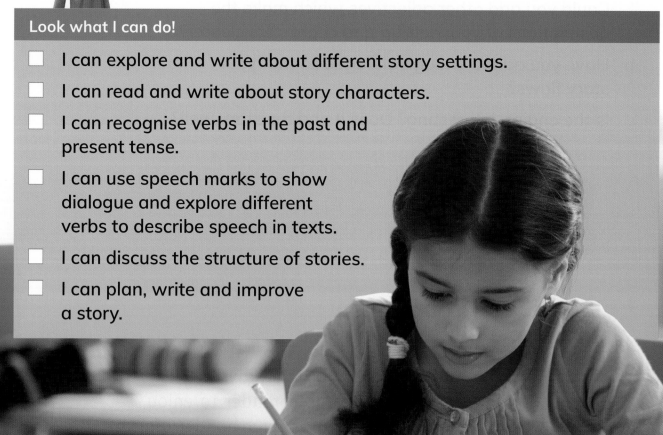

Look what I can do!

- ☐ I can explore and write about different story settings.
- ☐ I can read and write about story characters.
- ☐ I can recognise verbs in the past and present tense.
- ☐ I can use speech marks to show dialogue and explore different verbs to describe speech in texts.
- ☐ I can discuss the structure of stories.
- ☐ I can plan, write and improve a story.

Check your progress

1 Write three sentences describing this setting.

2 Choose a character in the picture.
Write a character description about the person you have chosen.

3 Copy the table into your notebook and write these words in the table.

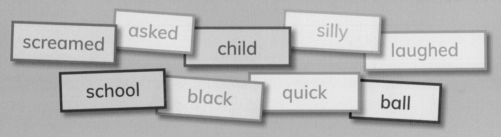

Nouns	Verbs	Adjectives

4 Look at these sentences about dialogue.
Copy the true sentences in your notebook.

a Dialogue is what characters in a story do.

b Dialogue is what characters in a story say.

c We put speech marks around words like 'he said' so we know who is talking.

d We put speech marks around words which characters actually say.

Projects

Group project: Imagine you are able to interview Roald Dahl. Do some research about him. Write eight questions you would ask him. Act the interview with Roald Dahl. Take turns to be the interviewer and Roald.

Pair project: Choose a name and write adjectives you would use to describe your character. Pretend to be your character for a partner or draw a picture of your character. Ask your partner to write adjectives that describe your character. Do their adjectives match the adjectives you wrote when you were creating your character? Now swap with your partner.

Solo project: Choose a photograph from home that shows a scene you know well and that reminds you of a happy time. Write a description of the scene and then write about that moment in time.

2   Let's have a party

❯ 2.1   Looking at celebrations

We are going to...

- research what a celebration is.

Getting started

1. Look at the photographs of celebrations.
2. What different celebrations do they show?
3. Talk about the photographs.

1 Talk about a celebration you have been to. Remember to include:

- why you were celebrating
- what you did
- where you were
- when it happened
- who else was there.

2 Find out about celebrations. Use a dictionary to find the **definition** of *celebration*.

3 Find out more about celebrations.

a Do an internet search and look in books.

b How many different types of celebration can you list?

Listening tip

Take turns when listening to other people. Listen carefully to what they are saying and ask questions. Have you been to similar celebrations?

Key word

definition: the meaning of a word

> 2.2 Writing lists

We are going to...

- write lists to plan a party.

Getting started

1 With a partner, talk about a party you have been to.

2 Ask each other four questions about the party.

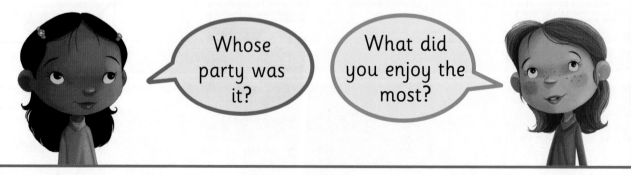

Whose party was it?

What did you enjoy the most?

1 Plan a class party!

a In a small group, talk about:

- what you need to do before a party
- how you will tell people there is a party
- what you could do at the party.

b Write a list of the ideas you have discussed.

Number the items on your list in the order that things need to be done.

> **Writing tip**
>
> You usually write lists of things down the page, not across the page.

2 Can you remember all we have learnt about verbs?

Look back at Session 1.7 if you need reminding.

a Answer these questions in your notebook.

- What is a verb?
- Why do we use verbs?
- Can we write a sentence without using a verb?

b Copy these sentences. <u>Underline</u> the verb in each one.

- Write ideas for a class party.
- Send invitations to the party.
- Parties are fun!
- Some people dance at parties.

> 2.3 Fiction or non-fiction?

We are going to...

- **discuss the difference between fiction and non-fiction.**

Getting started

There are two main types of writing:

| fiction | non-fiction |

These are called text types.

1 Discuss what you think fiction is.

2 Discuss what you think non-fiction is.

3 Say an example of each text type.

Key words

fiction: a story or text that someone has made up

non-fiction: a text giving information or telling the reader true things

1 Look at ten different books. Sort them into piles of fiction and non-fiction books. Discuss how you know which books go in which pile.

Reading tip

If you don't know whether a book is fiction or non-fiction, try these steps to help you decide.

1 Look at the title. The titles of non-fiction books usually tell you what the book is about; fiction books may have more imaginative titles.

2 Look at the pictures on the cover. Non-fiction books may have photographs or realistic pictures.

3 Read the blurb. The blurb on the back cover tells you the subject of the book if it is non-fiction, or what the story is about if it is fiction.

4 Flick through the book. Does it have a contents page or index? Are there headings above short paragraphs of writing? If so, it's probably a non-fiction book.

How are we doing?

Ask your partner to check your piles of books. They can draw you a smiley face if you have got the books all in the right piles, or a sad face if you need to change some.

2 Read texts 1–3.

  a Are the texts fiction or non-fiction? Look at how the texts are set out and what clues this might give you.

[1] # A surprise

João was excited. Vovó was going to be 80 and his family was planning to have a surprise party for her. He had known his grandmother was old, but not that old! He wondered what old people did at parties. They couldn't dance or play games. Perhaps they just ate and talked. Suddenly, he felt less excited. But this was going to be a surprise party. He wondered what he could do to surprise her. He knew she loved cakes so he thought he might make her one.

[2]

How to make a sponge cake

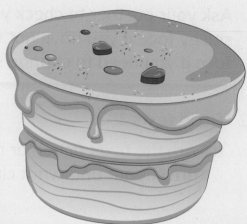

You will need:

- 175 g softened butter, sugar and flour
- 3 medium eggs
- 1 tsp baking powder
- sweets and coloured icing

What to do:

1 First, mix together the butter and the sugar.

2 Add the eggs and beat until smooth and creamy.

3 Now, mix the baking powder with the flour.

4 Then, sift the flour into the butter mix and gently mix in.

5 Finally, spoon the mixture into two shallow cake tins and bake in a medium oven for 25 minutes.

6 When the cake is cool, decorate it with sweets and coloured icing.

[3]

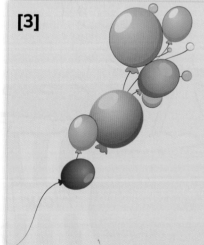

Amelia

You are invited to: Vovó's Surprise Party.

It will be at: Santa Teresa Colombo Café,

Rio de Janeiro

On: 18 May at 4.30.

Come dressed to impress.

RSVP

b   Answer these questions.

- Which text is an invitation? Which text is a story? Which text gives instructions?

- Talk about the differences between the texts. Talk about the features of each text type.

- Write a list of the main features of each text type.

3 Answer these questions.

a Who is Vovó?

b What does João think he will surprise Vovó with?

c Do you think João will enjoy Vovó's party?

d Why do you think João suddenly felt less excited?

e When you make the cake, what must you do after you beat the eggs?

f In which city will Vovó's party be held?

〉 2.4 Following instructions

We are going to...

- follow instructions and recognise the role of command verbs and sequencing words.

Getting started

1 Continue to plan your class party.

Discuss:

- Why are you having a party?

- Will the party have a theme?

- Who will you invite to the party?

2 Make notes about the things you discuss.

1 Look at these instructions for making a pop-up card.
Read the instructions to yourself and then answer the questions.

How to make a pop-up card

You will need:

- pieces of card:

  - Card 1: 25 cm long, 20 cm wide

  - Card 2: 12 cm long, 8 cm wide

  - Card 3: 12 cm square

- scissors

- a ruler

- glue

- colouring pens or pencils

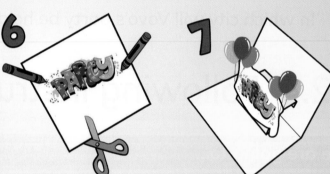

1 First, fold Card 1 in half.

2 Then, draw a line 1 cm from either end of Card 2.

3 Fold Card 2 along both the lines and then fold it in half.

4 Next, open Card 1.

5 Glue along the ends of Card 2, then stick Card 2 inside Card 1, as shown in the picture.

6 Draw a party picture on Card 3 and cut it out.

7 Finally, glue your party picture onto the edge of Card 2.

a What type of text is this?

b Why does it help to have a 'You will need' section?

c How do the pictures help?

d Why do you think the numbers are important?

2 Now follow the instructions in Activity 1 to make your own pop-up card. Put your card somewhere safe. You will need it in the next session.

How am I doing?

Look at the card you have made.
What could you have done to improve it?

Were the instructions to make the card clear? How could you change the instructions to make them easier to understand?

3 Good instructions are clear and easy to follow.
The sentences use a special form of the verb.

a Look again at the instructions for making a pop-up card in Activity 1. Find all the verbs. Where are they in the sentence? Write a list of the verbs.

b Now find all the other words at the beginning of the sentences. Make a list of these words too.

Language focus

The form of the verb used in instruction texts is sometimes called a **command** or **imperative verb** because it tells, or commands, you to do something, such as *draw, open* or *fold*. It is a 'bossy' verb.

Words such as *first, next* and *finally* tell you the order to do things in. They are called **sequencing words**.

Instructions usually begin with a command verb or a sequencing word.

> 2.5 Writing an invitation

We are going to...

- write an invitation.

Getting started

1 Look back at the invitation to Amelia in Session 2.3, Activity 2.

2 Talk about the invitation:

- Whose party is it?

- Where does the party take place?

- What time does the party start?

- How do we know the party is happening in the future? Which words give us that information?

Amelia
You are invited to: Vovó's Surprise Party.
It will be at: Santa Teresa Colombo Café, Rio de Janeiro
On: 18 May at 4.30.
Come dressed to impress.
RSVP

1 How do you know the text to Amelia is an invitation?

a Talk about the layout – where the writing is on the page. Why isn't it all on one line?

b Discuss the order the information is given in.

c What other information is included in the invitation? What do the letters RSVP (répondez s'il vous plaît) mean?

d Make a list of the important information you need to include in your class party invitation.

2 You are now ready to write your invitation.

a First, write your invitation in rough. Think about the layout and the order you give the information in.

b Use a computer to type your final invitation or write it in neat, clear handwriting.

c   When you have finished your invitation, print it and/or
    cut it out. Stick it carefully on the front of the pop-up card
    you made in Session 2.4.

How are we doing?

Show your invitation to a partner. Ask them what they think
you have done well and what they think you might change.

3   Listen carefully to what Tuhil says to Anya. He is
    inviting her to his party. Write an invitation from Tuhil
    to Anya. Make sure you include all the important
    information you have heard in their conversation.

4   Look at these sentences.

The family are **inviting** people to Vovó's
Surprise Party.

Amelia has been **invited** to Vovó's
Surprise Party.

Language focus

Before adding –*ing* or –*ed* to a word, look at the letter before
the last letter to see if it is a consonant or a vowel.

- If it is a consonant, just add –*ing* or –*ed*, but if the last letter
  is an e, remove the e before adding –*ing* or –*ed*.

Example: *call* = *calling*   *invite* = *inviting*

- If it is a *single* vowel, just double the last letter before adding –*ing*
  or –*ed*, but don't double the last letter if the word ends in w, x or y.

Example: *stir* = *stirring*   *play* = *playing*

- If there are two vowel letters, just add –*ing* or –*ed*.

Example: *beep* = *beeping*

a   Add –ed to each of these words.
    Don't forget the rules!

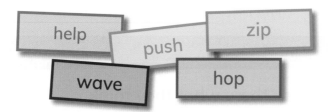

help   push   zip   wave   hop

b   Add –ing to each of these words.
    Don't forget the rules!

sit   sweep   wait   bake   box

> **Key words**
>
> **consonant:** all the letters in the alphabet that aren't a vowel, for example, b, c, d, f and g
>
> **vowel:** the letters a, e, i, o and u (y is called a semi-vowel because it sometimes acts as a vowel, for example, *fly*)

> 2.6 Following and writing instructions

We are going to...

- **follow and write instructions.**

Getting started

Instructions tell us how to do something.

1   Write a list of activities where we need to follow instructions.

INSTRUCTIONS

- Read through the enclosed assembly instruction carefully before assembling the plane.

- Carefully push out each pre-stamped part from the wood board with your fingernails, begining with the thinner parts.

2   Share your list with others.
    Have you all written the same types of instructions?

1 Look at the instructions for walking from a school to a nearby playground.

How to get from school to the playground

1 Leave school by the front gates.

2 Turn right and walk towards the crossroads.

3 Cross the road carefully at the traffic lights.

4 Walk along the small lane opposite the shop that runs next to the stream.

5 Next, go over the bridge.

6 Turn left into the park. The playground can be found nearby.

These instructions are often called **directions**.

The instructions use:

- short sentences
- simple sentences
- ordered sentences
- command verbs.

Glossary

directions: instructions for getting from one place to another

Writing tip

Instructions need to be easy to read, easy to understand and easy to follow. When we write instructions, we use short, simple sentences and put them in the correct order. Remember, instructions also include command verbs and sequencing words so the reader can easily see what needs to be done.

2 Think about the directions you would give someone coming to your class party. Write instructions for walking from the school gate to the room the party will be held in.

a Think carefully about the route you are going to describe in your instructions.

b Think about the order people need to read the instructions to understand the route.

c Write the instructions. Remember to include command verbs and sequencing words.

Key word

compound words: two smaller words put together to make one bigger word, for example, *play* + *ground* = *playground*

3 What are compound words?

a Look at this word. What do you notice about it?

playground

b Use these words to make as many compound words as you can.

Example: *bedroom*

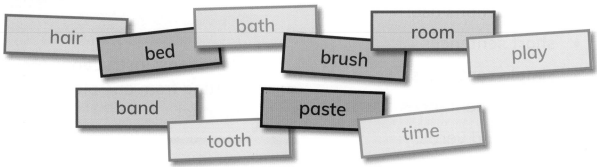

hair
bath
room
bed
brush
play
band
paste
tooth
time

Reading tip

Be aware of compound words when you're reading – it can make long words easier to read. Look for words with unusual strings of consonants, for example bookcase, seatbelt, popcorn and football.

Writing tip

Compound words are easy to spell – you just spell
the two shorter words one after the other.

c   Now look at these words. How many compound words can you make?

every   any   thing   one   some

no   where   how   body

〉 2.7 Contents pages and indexes

We are going to...

- use a contents page and an index.

Getting started

In a group, discuss these questions:

1   Do you enjoy party food?
2   What is your favourite type of party food?
3   What do you like to drink at parties?
4   Have you ever been to a party that doesn't have food?

1   What would you like to eat at your class party?

a   Talk about the food you could have at your party.
Make a list of party food you would like to have.

b   What kind of book would tell you how to make the food?
Where could you find the book?

2 Read the text.

Fruit rockets

You will need:

- A slice of watermelon, about 1 cm thick

- strawberries

- half a small banana

- a slice of pineapple

- 3 wooden skewers.

Method:

1 First, cut the watermelon into three triangles.
Cut the top point off each triangle.

2 Push a piece of watermelon onto a skewer.
This is the base of your rocket.

3 Next, cut the strawberries in half.

4 Push half a strawberry onto the skewer, above the watermelon.

5 Then, cut down the middle of the banana.
Cut off slices about 2 cm long and thread them
onto the skewer above the strawberry.

6 Finally, cut the pineapple slice into triangles.
Place a triangle, point up, at the top of the rocket.

7 Make two more rockets.

8 Serve immediately.

a What type of text is this? How do you know?

b What sort of book does the page come from?

3 Look at this contents page and index.

Contents
Healthy drinks

Healthy snacks

Index

a Discuss what is the same and what is different about the contents page and index. When would you use each page? Which kind of book do you think they come from?

b Find a book with a contents page and index. Choose a topic to look up in the book. Use the contents page and index to help you.

Key words

contents page: a page at the front of a book that shows you where you can find different chapters or sections

index: an alphabetical list at the back of a book that shows you which page to find information of interest

Reading tip

Use your knowledge of the alphabet to help you find information quickly with an index.

How do you work out whether to use the contents page or the index to find information in a book?

4   Find some recipes for party snacks in books or on the internet.

   a   Add one or two more items to the list of party food you made in Activity 1.

   b   Make a note of where you found the recipes.

> 2.8 Making lists

We are going to...

- **write lists.**

Getting started

Lists can help us remember things. Write a list about everything you need to remember to do when you get home from school today.

Remember, lists are usually written down the page, not across the page. This makes each point in a list clear and easy to identify.

1 You've decided to make fruit rockets using the recipe in Session 2.7, Activity 2, but you don't have everything you need. Don't worry, you can go shopping!

   a   Write a list of items you need to buy. Think about the layout of your list.

   b   Rewrite your list in alphabetical order.

Don't forget to buy the skewers!

2 Look at your list of party food ideas from Session 2.7.

   a   Choose one of the snacks on your list and find the recipe you need to make it.

   b   Which ingredients do you have to buy? Write a shopping list.

3 Write your own recipe. It can be a made-up recipe or something you just enjoy eating or drinking.

   a   Look at the layout of the 'Fruit rockets' recipe in Session 2.7, Activity 2. Write your recipe in the same way.

Remember, good instructions are short, simple sentences that use command verbs and sequencing words.

   b   First, write a list of the things and ingredients you need. Use the title: You need.

   c   Then, write instructions on how to make your recipe. Use the title: Method.

2.9 Giving instructions

We are going to...

- **speak fluently and confidently when giving instructions.**

Getting started

1 Look at these photographs of children playing games.

2 Discuss the games they are playing.

3 Have you played these games?

4 Would they be good games for your class party?

1 In a group, discuss the games you each enjoy playing. As a group, choose three games you would like to play at your party.

2 Look again at the different types of instructions in this unit. Write a list of everything you need to remember when you write instructions.

   a In a coloured pen, <u>underline</u> everything that would be the same if you spoke rather than wrote instructions.

   b In a different coloured pen, add anything that you'd do differently if people could only hear your instructions and not read them.

Listening tip

Remember, when working in a group, everyone must listen to each other and respect each other's ideas (even if you don't agree!).

3 Practise giving instructions for a simple game.
Think about how you speak when you give instructions.

Speaking tip

Speak clearly; don't speak too quietly or too fast.

❯ 2.10 Planning a game

We are going to...

- plan and discuss a new party game.

Getting started

Read the instructions for how to play Fruit Basket.

How to play Fruit Basket

What you need:

Exactly nine players

1 Divide the players into groups of three.

2 Name each group a type of fruit, for example, *banana, pineapple.*

3 Mix the players up and place the players in a circle around a central point.

4 Choose one player to stand in the middle of the circle.

5 The player in the middle then calls out the name of one of the groups, for example, 'Pineapple!' Everyone in that group must now move to a different place in the circle as quickly as they can. The player who is the last to a place now has to stand in the middle of the circle.

6 If the player in the middle wants to do something different, they can call out 'Fruit basket!' That means everyone has to find a new position in the circle.

7 When the game finishes, you do not want to be the one in the middle!

1 Try playing the game. Do the instructions make sense? Could they be improved?

2 Invent a party game!

a Talk about how you could change or improve a party game you already know.

b Plan the party game.
   Make notes about how to play the new game.

   • What equipment do you need?

   • How many people can play?

   • How do you play the game?

Don't try to change too much. Just change one or two things that will make the game more fun to play.

3 Practise saying your instructions for your new game aloud.

 a Use your notes to help you when you speak.

 b Try teaching your game to others.
 Ask them how they might improve your game.

How am I doing?

How could you improve your instructions?
Write any new ideas with your notes.

〉 2.11 Writing instructions

We are going to...

- **use sequencing words and command verbs to write instructions.**

Getting started

Write a checklist of everything you need to remember when writing a set of instructions for a party game.

1 Write instructions for the party game you invented in Session 2.10, Activity 2.

 As you write, think about your readers.

 - Are you giving them enough information?

 - Are the instructions in the correct order?

 - Do the instructions begin with a sequencing word or a command verb?

2 Tick (✔) each item on the checklist from the Getting started activity as you write your instructions.

> 2.12 Improving your instructions

We are going to...

- improve the instructions we have written.

Getting started

1   Re-read the instructions you wrote in Session 2.11.

2   Read the instructions aloud to yourself. Do they make sense?

1   Proofread your instructions. Check:

- the grammar (Does it make sense?)

- the spelling (Use a dictionary for any words you aren't sure about.)

- the punctuation (Have you used full stops and capital letters in the correct places?).

How am I doing?

How can your instructions be improved? Have you written the steps of the game in the correct order? Do you need to add any sequencing words? Have you used command verbs?

2 Write the final instructions for your game.
Make sure your handwriting is neat and tidy.

3 In groups, take turns to play each other's games.
Are the instructions easy to follow?

Speaking tip

Speak slowly and clearly as you read out your instructions.
This will help others to follow them.

Look what I can do!

☐ I can write lists.

☐ I can discuss the difference between fiction and non-fiction.

☐ I can use a contents page and index.

☐ I can follow instructions and recognise the role of command verbs
and sequencing words.

☐ I can speak fluently and confidently when giving instructions.

☐ I can write instructions and improve them.

Check your progress

1 In this unit you have read instructions for making:

- a cake
- a pop-up card
- some fruit rockets.

Write a list of all the things that are the same about these instructions.

2 What other non-fiction texts are in this unit?

3 Write two sentences, each starting with a command verb.

4 Finish these compound words.

a foot_____   b any_____

Continued

5 Complete these word sums.

    a   walk + –ing = _____

    b   smile + –ed = _____

    c   sit + –ing = _____

Projects

Group project: Write your own recipe for something you love to eat. It could be something you create yourself. As a group, discuss how you are going to display your recipes to create a recipe book.

Pair project: Imagine you and a partner are running the class party. Write a list of everything that needs to be done on the day. Then write the things on your list in the order they need to be done, starting with what you need to do first.

Solo project: Write instructions on how to care for an animal. You are going away for the weekend to a family party and a friend is coming to look after your animal. Write instructions on how they should care for them.

3 ▶ Poems from around the world

〉 3.1 Words that make pictures

We are going to...

- **read and answer questions about a poem from Bahamas.**

Getting started

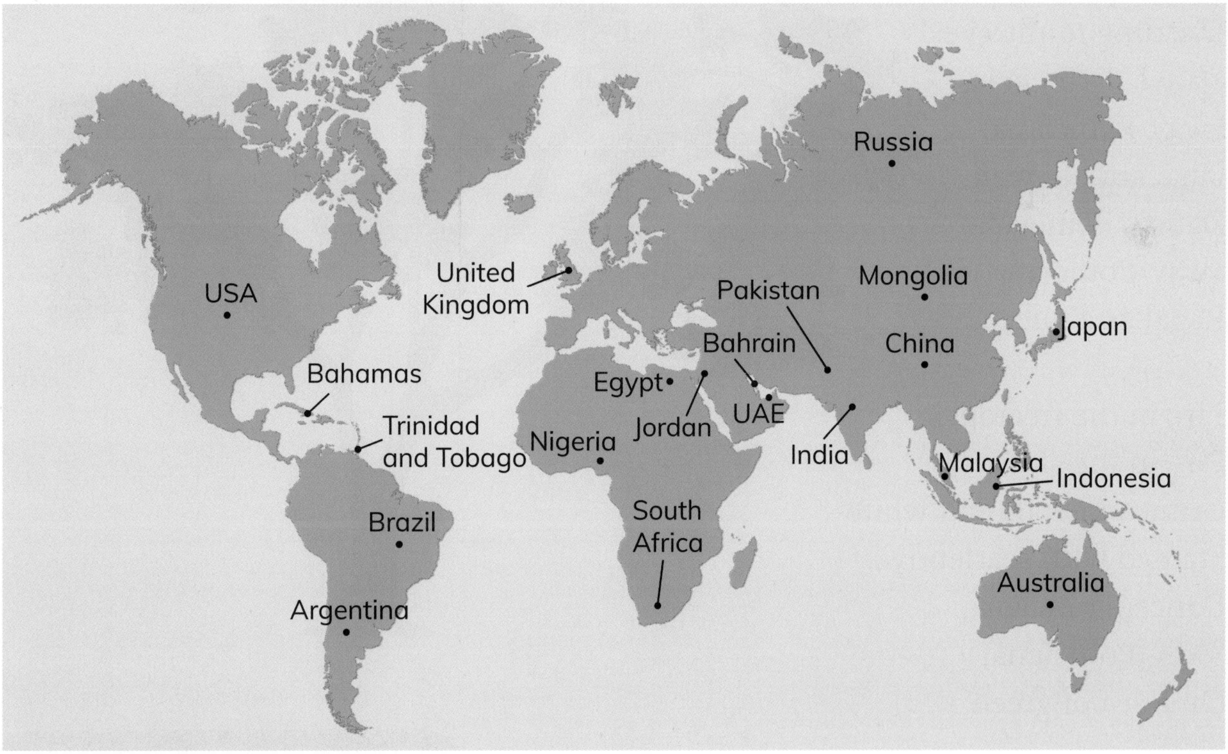

1 Can you find the country you live in?
2 How many other countries, that haven't already been named, can you list?
3 What do you know about the countries you can name?

1 When you read a poem, do you always know which country it is from?

   a Talk about the clues you might find in a poem to tell you which country the poem was written in. If a poem was from your town, region or country, what would it say?

   b Read *Dancing Poinciana* by Telcine Turner. Can you guess who or what Poinciana is?

   c *Dancing Poinciana* is a poem from Bahamas. Find Bahamas on the map.

Dancing Poinciana

Fire in the treetops,
Fire in the sky.
Blossoms red as sunset
Dazzling to the eye.
Dance, Poinciana,
Sway, Poinciana,
On a sea of green.
Dance, Poinciana,
Sway, Poinciana,
Regal as a queen.

Fire in the treetops,
Fire in the sky.
Crimson petals and white
Stained with scarlet dye.
Dance, Poinciana,
Sway, Poinciana,
On a sea of green.

Dance, Poinciana,
Sway, Poinciana,
Regal as a queen.

Telcine Turner

Glossary

regal: special like royalty, noble

Reading tip

If you don't know what a word means, don't give up reading! You can:

- think of another word that looks the same (for example, *stained* looks like *stain*)
- read the rest of the sentence and see if you can work out the word
- look at the pictures – can you find information from them?
- ask someone or look the word up in a dictionary.

2 Some of the words in *Dancing Poinciana* tell you about Bahamas, where the poem comes from. Some of the words make pictures in your head.

   a Which words in the poem tell you about Bahamas?

   b Which words help you see a picture of the tree in your head?

   c What do you think of the poem? Can you tell where it comes from? Can you see the tree?
   Write about what the poem makes you think and see.

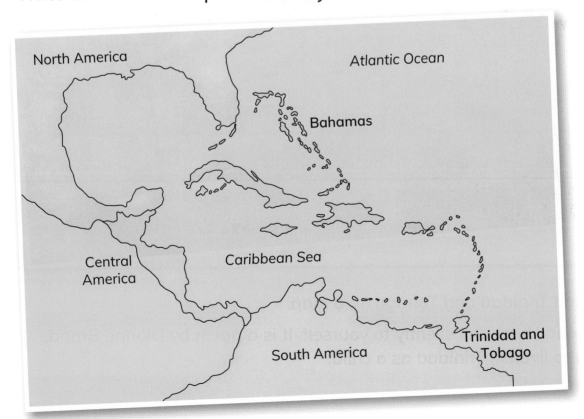

> 3.2 Reading with expression

We are going to...

- **read aloud with expression.**

Getting started

1 What is a hurricane?

2 Have you ever been in a hurricane?

3 These photos show what happens in a hurricane.

   Talk about how it would feel to be in a hurricane.

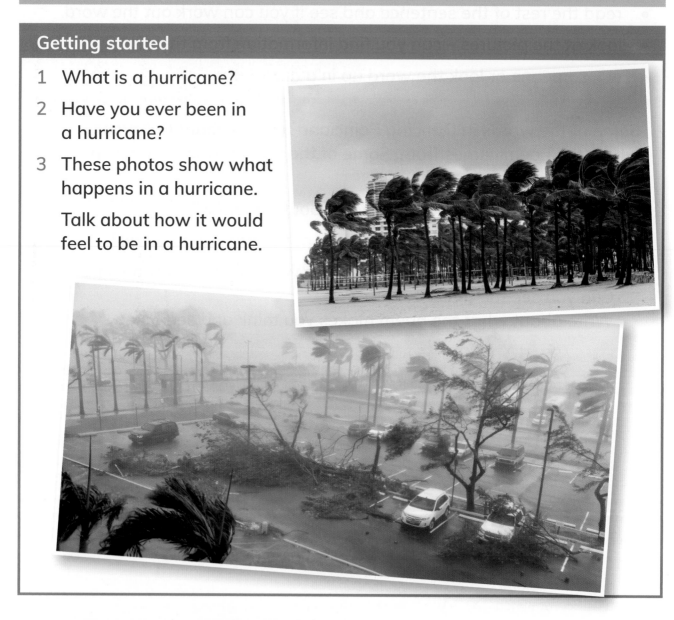

1 Find Trinidad and Tobago on a map.

   Read *Hurricane* silently to yourself. It is a poem by Dionne Brand, who lived in Trinidad as a child.

Hurricane

Shut the windows
Bolt the doors
Big rain coming
Climbing up the mountain

Neighbours whisper
Dark clouds gather
Big rain coming
Climbing up the mountain

Gather in the clothesline
Pull down the blinds
Big wind rising
Coming up the mountain

Branches falling
Raindrops flying

Treetops swaying
People running
Big wind blowing
Hurricane! on the mountain.

Dionne Brand

a   List three signs in the weather that tell people that
    the hurricane is coming.

b   List three things people do to make their houses ready
    for the hurricane.

c   Look at the last verse again.
    Write why you think the people are running.

d   How does this poem interest the reader?

2 Practise adding –ing to verbs.

    a Copy the verbs in the poem that end in –ing.

    b Now write the verbs without the suffix –ing.

       Example: *coming* = *come.*

Language focus

To change a verb (an action word) into the present tense:

- For most **verbs**, just add –*ing* to the end of the verb.

- For verbs that end in e, take off the e and then add –*ing.*

- For verbs that have a short vowel followed by one consonant, double the consonant and then add –*ing.*

3 *Hurricane* is a good poem to perform.

    a Practise reading the poem aloud. Use your voice to make the poem sound interesting to people listening.

    b Perform the poem in a group.

Speaking tip

Preparing to perform:

- Make sure you understand what the poem means.

- Check that you can read all the words.

- Decide what kind of voice you will read with: *Happy? Sad? Urgent? Slow?*

- Think about how fast or how slowly you will read.

- Look for punctuation marks – they can help you to understand which words go together.

- Decide which words are the important ones in each line and make sure you say them clearly.

❯ 3.3 Performing a poem

We are going to...

- **perform a poem which includes powerful words and noun phrases.**

Getting started

1 What do you know about the country of Mongolia?

2 In pairs, try to find two facts about Mongolia.

3 Share your facts with the rest of the class.

In Mongolian myths, dragons are linked to water, thunder, lightning and the power of the Earth.

1 Read this traditional poem from Mongolia.

The Thunder is a Great Dragon

The thunder is a great dragon that lives in the water and flies in the air.
He carries two stones.
When he strikes them together, the lightning flashes and the thunder roars.
The dragon **pursues** the spirits of evil, and wherever he finds them, he **slays** them.
The evil spirits hide in the trees, and the dragon destroys them.

Traditional

Glossary

pursues: tries to catch

slays: attacks

   a Now read the poem aloud with expression.

   b Discuss the poem and how it might be linked to Mongolia.

   c Talk about what happens in the poem.
      Which words make pictures in your head?

   d How does this poem get the attention of the reader?

2 Work in groups. Plan a short performance about the poem
    The Thunder is a Great Dragon. Present your performance.

What did you do to make your performance exciting
for the audience to watch?

3 Poems often use powerful words and noun phrases.

> **Language focus**
>
> A **noun phrase** is a group of words that are used instead of a noun.
>
> A noun phrase can be replaced by a pronoun.
>
> his huge, leathery wings ⟶ they
>   noun phrase   pronoun
>
> Notice how adjectives describe the noun in this noun phrase.

   a Write your own short poem explaining another way the
      dragon could make thunder. Think of some powerful words
      and noun phrases to use in your poem. Remember that your
      poem doesn't have to rhyme.

   b Publish your poem. Write your poem in your best
      handwriting or produce a final version on a computer
      so it can be displayed.

› 3.4 Onomatopoeia

We are going to...

- **recognise onomatopoeic words and include some in a new verse of a poem.**

Getting started

1 Find Africa on the world map in Session 3.1.

2 Now find the Congo River on this map.

3 Can you see where the Congo River should be on the world map?

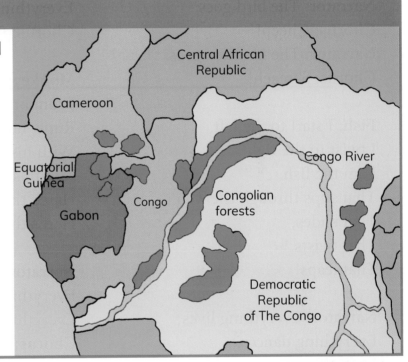

Key word

onomatopoeia:
when a word mimics or describes a sound of the object or action it is about

Did you know that the Congo River is the deepest river and the ninth longest river in the world? It winds through a huge rainforest where many colourful animals live.

1 Read the poem *Song of the Animal World*.
It describes the way animals move in the forest and the sound they make.
How many movement verbs can you count in the poem?

Song of the Animal World

Narrator: The fish goes
Chorus: Plop!
Narrator: The bird goes
Chorus: Cheep!
Narrator: The monkey goes
Chorus: Screech!

Fish: I start to the left,
I twist to the right.
I am the fish
That slips through the water,
That slides,
That twists,
That leaps!

Narrator: Everything lives,
Everything dances,
Everything sings.
Chorus: Plop! Cheep! Screech!

Bird: The bird flies away,
Flies, flies, flies,
Goes, returns, passes,
Climbs, floats, swoops.
I am the bird!

Narrator: Everything lives,
Everything dances,
Everything sings.
Chorus: Plop! Cheep! Screech!

Monkey: The monkey!
From branch to branch
Runs, hops, jumps,
With his wife and baby,
Mouth stuffed full, tail in air,
Here's the monkey!
Here's the monkey!

Narrator: Everything lives,
Everything dances,
Everything sings.
Chorus: Plop! Cheep! Screech!

Traditional

2 Talk about the poem and how it is linked to the Congo, the place it comes from.

 a Discuss the sounds in the poem.
   What sound words are there?

 b Talk about movement in the poem.
   What movement words are there?

 c List three more onomatopoeic words linked with the sounds the animals in the poem might make.

 d Do you think this is a happy or sad poem?

Language focus

Onomatopoeia is when a word mimics or describes a sound of the object or action it is about. Onomatopoeia can bring a poem to life, as it has done in *Song of the Animal World.*

Example: **Narrator:** The fish goes

  Chorus: *Plop!*

  Narrator: The bird goes

  Chorus: *Cheep!*

  Narrator: The monkey goes

  Chorus: *Screech!*

Other examples of onomatopoeia are *slither*, *rustle*, *bang* and *buzz*.

Writing tip

Notice how the verb endings change depending on the noun or pronoun the verb goes with:

I **twist** to the right.

The fish **twists** to the right.

I **sing**.

Everything **sings**.

3 You are going to make up another verse for the poem.

a Copy the table. Fill it in using the information from the poem about the bird and the monkey.

b Think of another animal from Africa and the last row of the table.

You could choose a frog, a gorilla, a crocodile or a leopard – or a different animal.

c Make notes in the table about the sound the animal makes, where it lives and how it moves.

d Write a new verse about your animal.

Animal	How it sounds	Where it lives	How it moves	Other information
fish	Plop!	the water	twists, slips, slides, leaps	swims through the water
bird				
monkey				

> 3.5 Writing a haiku

We are going to...

- write a haiku.

Getting started

1 Find Japan on the world map in Session 3.1.

2 In a group, discuss what you already know about Japan.

3 What would you like to find out about the country?

Key word

haiku: a type of Japanese poem that has three lines and is made up of 17 syllables

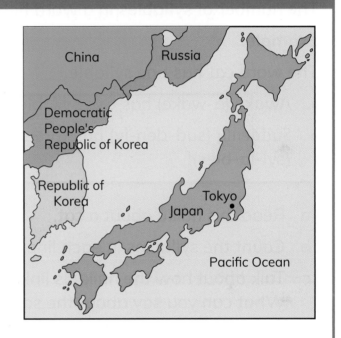

China   Russia

Democratic People's Republic of Korea

Republic of Korea   Tokyo   Japan

Pacific Ocean

Did you know that Japan is made up of a string of more than six thousand islands in East Asia. It is sometimes called the Land of the Rising Sun because its name in Japanese means 'the sun's origin'.

Did you know that many Japanese people are very fond of cats? There is even a national cat day!

1 Haikus are Japanese poems. They have a total of 17 syllables in three lines. There are five syllables in the first and last lines, and seven syllables in the middle line. Haikus are very short, but you should still be able to see a clear picture of the subject in your head when you read them.

Language focus

The number of **syllables** in a word helps give it rhythm.

Example:

The word *cat* has one syllable.

- *Awake* (a-wake) has two syllables and so does *stretching* (stre-tching).
- *Suddenly* (sud-den-ly) has three syllables – and so does *syllables* (syl-la-bles)!

a Read this haiku about a cat.

b Count the syllables in each line.

c Talk about how the haiku is linked to Japan.
What can you say about the sounds in the poem?

d Read the poem aloud with expression.

Suddenly awake.
Stretching, yawning, arching back,
stalking, pouncing: cat.

What helps you to work out the number of syllables in a word?

2 Listen carefully to a wildlife charity news report about the endangered tiger.

    a List three things you have heard about the tiger. Include adjectives.

    b Now write a short sentence about each of the three things.

    c Use these sentences to write a haiku about the tiger.

3 Write your own haiku.

    a Choose an animal to write your haiku about.

    b Write a list of adjectives that describe your animal.

    c Write three short sentences using some of the words you have listed.

    d Write your haiku. Give your haiku a title.

> Remember, there are three lines in a haiku; five syllables in the first line, seven syllables in the second line and five syllables in the third line.

How are we doing?

Read your haiku to a partner. Can they count the correct number of syllables in it? Do they like your haiku? Do they have any suggestions for how it might be improved?

> Remember, a haiku doesn't tell a story. It helps make a clear picture in your head of a subject.

> 3.6 Reviewing poems

We are going to...

- compare and review poems.

Getting started

1 Read through all the poems in this unit.

2 Remind yourself of where in the world they were written.

3 Which poem do you like the best?

1 Choose three of the poems in this unit to compare.

a Copy the table on the next page and fill it in with notes about each of your chosen poems.

b Are there any links between the poems?

c Which poem did you like best? Why?

Title	Country	Topic	Language	Interesting things
1				
2				
3				

2   Write a review of your favourite poem.

How am I doing?

Check your review. Have you said what you liked about the poem?
Did you explain how the poem is linked to the country it is from?
Have you commented on the pictures the poem makes in your head?
Did you write about the powerful or unusual words the poet has
chosen and the sounds they make?

3   Now get ready to perform your favourite poem.

   a   Read the poem aloud. Ask a partner to listen to you reading
       the poem and to suggest improvements you could make.

   b   Perform the poem.

Speaking tip

Practise reading the poem again and again.

- Read with expression.

- Use movement.

- Use your voice and your body to support the poem's meaning.

Look what I can do!

☐ I can read and answer questions about poems.

☐ I can read aloud with expression.

☐ I can write a poem that includes powerful words and noun phrases.

☐ I can recognise onomatopoeic words and include some in my own writing.

☐ I can write a haiku.

☐ I can compare and review poems.

Check your progress

1 In this unit you have read poems from around the world and explored how poets use words to make pictures and create sounds. Read the start of a poem, *Coral Reef* by Clare Bevan and answer the questions.

Coral Reef

I am a teeming city;
An underwater garden
Where fishes fly;
A lost forest
of skeleton trees;
A home for starry anemones;
A hiding place for frightened fishes;
A skulking place for prowling predators;
An alien world
Whose unseen monsters
Watch with luminous eyes.

Clare Bevan

Continued

2　How is the poem linked to a place?

3　Is it linked to a country?

4　Which words in the poem help to make a picture in your head?

5　Write:

- three nouns that helped you know about the place
- three adjectives that helped build up a picture of the place
- three different noun phrases from the poem.

6　Write an onomatopoeic word that could be associated with any fish.

7　How many syllables do these words have?

　　a　Bahamas　　　b　Caribbean　　　c　Mongolia　　　d　Africa

Projects

Group project: Create a class book of the haikus written in this unit. Illustrate the haikus. How will you organise the task in your group?

Pair project: With a partner, research other poems from around the world. Choose a poem you each like and discuss why you like it. Read your poems aloud to each other.

Solo project: Write a short poem about the country you live in. Describe your country in your poem. Your poem could rhyme but it doesn't have to.

4 Myths and legends

> ## 4.1 Looking at a traditional story

We are going to...

- read and answer questions about a traditional story.

Getting started

1 Talk about different types of stories.

2 List as many different types as you can.

What kind of stories do you enjoy?

I love fantasy stories.

3 Look at these book covers. Write a title for each story. What type of stories are they?

1 Storytelling is important because many people learn about their culture and history through stories.

Read this story from the Alabama Tribe of North America. It explains how people discovered fire.

Reading tip

Punctuation helps us to read a text. For example, if speech marks are used, they show us that the words are being said by a character.

Bear and Fire

In the beginning, Bear owned Fire. Fire warmed Bear and his people on cold days and it gave them light when the nights were long and dark. Bear always carried Fire with him.

One day, Bear and his people went to a forest. Bear put Fire down at the edge of the forest, then Bear and his people went deeper and deeper into the forest to look for food. Fire blazed up happily for a while until it had burned nearly all of its wood. It started to smoke and flicker, then it **dwindled** down and down. Fire was worried. It was nearly out. 'Feed me! Feed me!' shouted Fire. But Bear and his people had wandered deep into the forest, and they did not hear Fire's cries.

At that moment, Man came walking through the forest and saw the small, flickering Fire. 'Feed me! Feed me!' cried Fire.

'What should I feed you?' Man asked. He had never seen Fire before.'

'I eat sticks and logs,' Fire replied.

Glossary

dwindle: to get smaller

Man picked up a stick and gave it to Fire. Fire sent its flames flickering up the side of the stick until the stick started to burn. Man brought more and more sticks and Fire leapt and danced in delight. Man warmed himself by the blazing Fire, enjoying the colours of the flames and the hissing sound Fire made as it ate the wood. Man and Fire were very happy together and Man fed Fire sticks whenever it got hungry.

A long time later, Bear and his people came back to the edge of the forest, looking for Fire. Fire was angry when it saw Bear and it jumped and roared at him and drove him away. So from that day to this, Fire has belonged to Man.

S. E. Schlosser

2 Answer these questions.

a   How was Fire useful to Bear and his people?

b   Why do you think Bear didn't take Fire into the forest with him?

c   How did Man know what to feed Fire?

d   What did Man like about Fire?

e   Why do you think Fire wouldn't go back to Bear?

3 Discuss what you like about the story. Is there anything you don't like?

> 4.2 What is a myth?

We are going to...

- **recognise and discuss the features of a myth.**

Getting started

1   Work in a group.
    Discuss what you know about myths.

2   Now read this information.

Continued

A myth is a traditional story, written long ago. Myths were passed on from person to person by word of mouth. Myths often contain:

- characters named after an animal or something from the natural world

- information which explains **why** or **how** something is

- characters that are not of this world, such as gods and goddesses

- things that don't happen in the real world.

3   Have you read any myths?

4   If you have, what happens in them?

---

1   Read *Bear and Fire* again and answer these questions.

  a   Why is there only one Bear, one Man and one Fire?

  b   The story begins with *In the beginning*. When do you think that was?

  c   Do you think this is a true story? Give your reasons.

  d   Can you find any of the features of myths in *Bear and Fire*? Which ones?

2   Answer these questions about the characters in the story.

  a   What do you know about Fire from the story?

  b   Discuss these words and choose the three that best describe Fire.

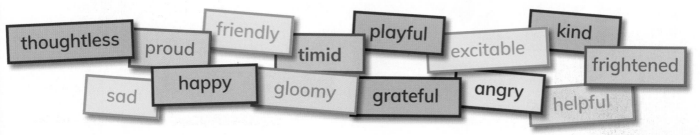

thoughtless   proud   friendly   timid   playful   excitable   kind   frightened   sad   happy   gloomy   grateful   angry   helpful

c Choose three words that you would use to describe Man.

d Choose three words that you would use to describe Bear.

e Write a noun phrase about each of the three characters.

Writing tip

Remember, a noun phrase is a phrase that acts like a noun and can be replaced by a pronoun, for example *the* kind *man* can be replaced with *he*.

3 Perform the story in groups.
First decide who is going to play which character and then act the story. Be aware of your audience.
Make the characters interesting to watch.
Remember the words you used to describe each character in Activity 2 to help create the characters.

> 4.3 Looking at pronouns

We are going to...

- **identify and use pronouns.**

Getting started

1 What is a noun?

2 Which of these words are nouns?

long night food hungry it

eat forest look bear flame

3 List five more nouns.

4 List five proper nouns.

5 How do we recognise proper nouns?

1 Read the Language focus box.

Language focus

Pronouns can be used instead of *nouns* or *noun phrases*.

Example nouns: *Bear, Fire, forest, stick*

Example noun phrases: *Bear and his people, small, flickering fire*

Example pronouns: *I, he, she, it, you, him, her, they, them*

Bear is looking. **He** is looking.

noun   pronoun

Using pronouns helps your writing flow.

Copy these sentences. <u>Underline</u> the pronoun or pronouns in each one.

a   Fire warmed Bear and his people, and it also gave them light.

b   Bear put Fire down and left it behind while he went to look for food.

c   When it had burned up all its wood, Fire started to call for help.

d   Man heard it. He came to help and he fed it sticks.

2   Re-read *Bear and Fire*. How many different pronouns can you find in the story? Make a list of the pronouns.

How do you recognise pronouns in a sentence?

3   Write three sentences about the story of *Bear and Fire*.
Each sentence must use at least one pronoun.
<u>Underline</u> the pronouns in your sentences.

Example: *Bear owned Fire first and carried <u>it</u> with <u>him</u> all the time.*

〉 4.4 What is a legend?

We are going to...

- **recognise and discuss the features of a legend.**

Getting started

1 Read this information about legends.

Legends often contain:

- a hero or heroine as the main character
- a dangerous task (sometimes involving a monster or a powerful enemy)
- an event in the past that is true or was possibly true, or an event linked to a culture or a set of beliefs.

Key word

legend: a traditional story, passed on from person to person by word of mouth

2 Work in a group. Discuss the similarities and differences between legends and myths.

---

1 Read the legend of *Mulan*. List which features of legends you can find in the story.

Mulan

Early one morning, Mulan was working quietly on her weaving **loom**. Mulan's father was ill in bed, her mother was cooking and her little brother was happily playing with his toys. Mulan sighed.

'Why are you sighing?' asked Mulan's mother.

'I saw a poster in town. Our country is being threatened and one man from each family must go and fight in the **Emperor**'s army!' said Mulan. She looked at her ill father who was far too weak to fight. Then she looked at her little brother; he was far too young to fight. Suddenly Mulan had an idea.

'I'm just the right age to fight. I have practised fighting with Father and I should be the one to join the army,' she said. 'I will dress like a boy and no one will know that I'm a girl.'

But her family did not agree. They tried to stop her but before they knew it, she had gone out and bought a speedy horse and a full set of protective **armour**.

At dawn she said goodbye to her family. She tied her hair up so she looked like a boy. Her family thought she would be back by the evening, but they were wrong. Three days later Mulan arrived at the army camp. She was nervous that the guard would notice she was a girl so she used her deepest voice. Mulan found army life hard. The days and nights were long and exhausting. She missed her family, but she didn't give up. She worked very hard to train for battle.

Soon it was time for Mulan's first battle. Although she was scared, she was as brave as any of the other soldiers. She used her sword with skill, but she also used her brain to confuse her enemy with tricks. Her fellow soldiers were very impressed and still none of them guessed that she was a girl.

Time passed and Mulan was in the army for ten long years. She became a well-known officer who led her troops into many winning battles, but she still missed her family. When the war was won, the Emperor was very pleased with Mulan and said she could have any reward. She knew what she wanted – her family and home! The Emperor agreed to her wish and sent her home, followed by her troops.

When she arrived, her family were very happy to see her. She went inside the house so she could let down her hair and put on a dress. As she appeared in front of her fellow troops they couldn't believe it. Mulan was a beautiful girl!

Her story travelled far and wide, across oceans and mountains, and it's still being told to this day.

Traditional, retold

Glossary

loom: equipment used for weaving threads into cloth

emperor: a ruler of an empire or country

armour: a strong covering that can protect the body

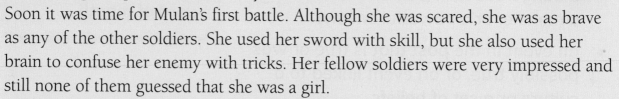

Mulan is an ancient Chinese legend.

2   Answer these questions about the story of *Mulan*
    in Activity 1.

    a Why did Mulan choose to join the army?

    b What two things did Mulan do so that others believed
    she was a boy?

    c Write three words that describe how Mulan might have
    felt during the first battle.

    d If you were Mulan, how would you have felt standing in
    front of your troops as a girl?

    e Do you think Mulan was wise? Why?

3   Look again at the story of Mulan in Activity 1. Look at Paragraph 1
    (*Early one morning ... protective* **armour**.) and list all the words you
    can find that have a suffix.

Language focus

A **suffix** is usually a group of letters that is put at the end of a word to
form a new word.

Example:

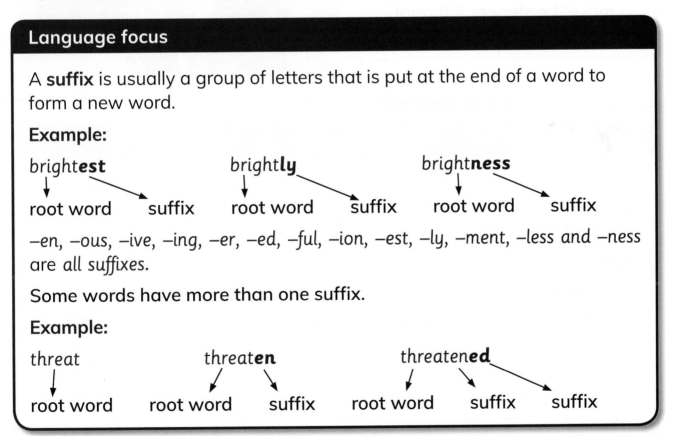

−en, −ous, −ive, −ing, −er, −ed, −ful, −ion, −est, −ly, −ment, −less and −ness
are all suffixes.

Some words have more than one suffix.

Example:

4   List five more words in the legend that include a suffix.
    How many different suffixes have you found?

> 4.5 Looking at paragraphs

We are going to...

- recognise paragraphs and understand how their openings establish links in a story.

Getting started

1 Do you remember what a paragraph is?

2 With a partner, look through a fiction and a non-fiction book, and talk about how paragraphs make the story or information easier to understand.

1 Read the Language focus box.

Language focus

A **paragraph** is a section of text. Each paragraph is a group of sentences about one idea or event. Each paragraph starts on a new line and is sometimes indented.

Example:

In the beginning, Bear owned Fire. Fire warmed Bear and his people on cold days and it gave them light when the nights were long and dark. Bear always carried Fire with him.

   One day, Bear and his people went to a forest. Bear put Fire down at the edge of the forest, then Bear and his people went deeper and deeper into the forest to look for food ...

Look back at *Bear and Fire* in Session 4.1, Activity 1.
How many paragraphs does the story have?

2   With a partner look again at *Bear and Fire* in Session 4.1, Activity 1.

   a   Copy the phrases at the beginning of each paragraph.

   b   Talk about what information the phrases give and how these words guide you through the story.

Remember, a phrase is a group of words.

Writing tip

Adverbs tell you how, where or when events take place.
Words such as *when*, *soon* and *after* are adverbs.

Phrases, or groups of words, such as *At long last* and *Over 3500 years ago* are short sentence openers, which act like adverbs.

---

3   Now look in detail at the paragraphs in *Mulan* in Session 4.4, Activity 1.

   a   Divide a large piece of paper into six boxes.
       Draw a line near the bottom of boxes 2–6 so labels can be added, as in Picture 1 box here.

Title of story Mulan	Picture 1	Picture 2
	Words or phrases Mulan looks at poster Decides to join army	Words or phrases
Picture 3	Picture 4	Picture 5
Words or phrases	Words or phrases	Words or phrases

b Re-read the story of *Mulan*.

- Decide which you think are the five most important events in the story.

- In the first box write the story title.

- In the following big boxes, draw pictures to show the events in the correct order.

Remember to plan what you will draw in each of the boxes before you begin to draw it.

c Re-read the story. Have you drawn one picture for each of the paragraphs?

d Write words or phrases describing what is happening in each paragraph under your pictures.

4 Look at the word or phrase at the beginning of each paragraph in *Mulan*. Copy the words or phrases. <u>Underline</u> any adverbs.

> 4.6 Joining sentences

We are going to...

- use connectives to write sentences with more than one clause.

Getting started

1 With a partner, list all the word classes you can remember, for example, *noun*.

2 Then write an example word for each word class.

noun = horse

1   Read the Language focus box.

> **Language focus**
>
> A **simple sentence** has only one action verb or verb phrase.
>
> A simple sentence has one clause.
>
> **Example:** Mulan's family did not agree.

List the subject and verb / verb phrase in each of these simple sentences.

   a   Mulan made up her mind.

   b   Mulan found army life hard.

   c   The battles were dangerous.

   d   Mulan walked out of her house as a girl.

2   Read the Language focus box.

> **Language focus**
>
> Simple sentences can be joined together using **connectives** to make **multi-clause sentences**.
>
> A multi-clause sentence has more than one clause:
>
> **Example:**
>
> She tied up her hair so she looked like a boy.
>
> clause   connective   clause
>
> Connectives can reflect time, place or cause.
>
> **Examples:**
>
> time connectives = first, next, last, then
>
> place connectives = up, over, behind
>
> cause connectives = so, if, because

Extend the four simple sentences to make more interesting multi-clause sentences, using the connectives in the boxes.

a   Mulan's family didn't want her to join the army

b   Mulan left home early one morning

c   Her family were very grateful.

d   Mulan arrived home

Writing tip

Sometimes nouns and pronouns are missed out in multi-clause sentences.

You could write:

She dressed as a boy soldier and she went off to join the army.

But it would be better to write:

She dressed as a boy soldier and went off to join the army.

---

3   Work with a partner to find more multi-clause sentences in the story of Mulan in Session 4.4, Activity 1.

a   Find five multi-clause sentences and write them in your notebook.

b   <u>Underline</u> the two clauses in each sentence and talk about how the sentences are joined.

> 4.7 Making links

We are going to...

- **identify, discuss and compare the differences between myths and legends.**

Getting started

1 Talk about the myth *Bear and Fire* in Session 4.1, Activity 1 and the legend of *Mulan* in Session 4.4, Activity 1.

2 Which was your favourite story? Why?

1 As a group, look back over the previous sessions on myths and legends. Discuss what you have learnt about the features of each type of text. Are there any features that link the different text types? Remind yourself of the features of each text type and talk about what is the same and what is different.

Listening tip

When you listen to others' thoughts about the stories, respond politely to those with a different point of view to yours.

2 Compare and contrast the two stories in this unit.

a Re-read the myth *Bear and Fire* from Session 4.1, Activity 1.

b Re-read the legend of *Mulan* from Session 4.4, Activity 1.

c Copy this table. Decide what is the same about the stories and what is different. Fill in your table.

	Myth *Bear and Fire*	Legend *Mulan*
When?		
Where?		
Characters		
Main event		
Theme/lesson	How people got fire	

3 Talk about the differences between legends and myths. Do you know any myths or legends in your history or culture? Are there stories about famous heroes or heroines who lived in your part of the world?

> 4.8 Rewriting a myth

We are going to...

- role play and write a re-telling of a myth.

Getting started

Write a list of as many different settings that you can think of in three minutes.

1   *Bear and Fire* is a well-known myth. Listen carefully to this version of the myth, then compare it to the myth in Session 4.1, Activity 1.

   a   List the things that are the same in the two stories.

   b   List the things that are different in the two stories.

   c   Does the second story still have all the features of a myth?

Check the information about myths in Session 4.2 Getting started to help you.

Listening tip

Listen carefully to the suggestions of others. Take turns to consider everyone's ideas.

2   Role play the story of *Bear and Fire* again, but this time imagine it is set in the present day. You can set the story wherever you want. Try a number of different settings. Talk about which setting makes the best story. You might choose to vary the characters, too.

3   The myth *Bear and Fire* has been re-told through the ages by many people.

   a   Make a storyboard for your own version of the myth.

   •   Choose a setting that you used for your role play to slightly change the story.

   •   Divide a piece of paper into six boxes. Write the title in the first box. Number the other boxes 1 to 5.

Key word

storyboard: a plan of what happens in a story

   •   Draw a picture and write notes in each numbered box to explain the story. Use each box to represent a new paragraph in the story.

b Now use the pictures and notes you have written to help explain your version of the myth to a partner.

How are we doing?

What parts of the story did your partner think were good?
What do they think could be improved? Did they enjoy the story?

> 4.9 Exploring a legend

We are going to...

- **read and answer questions about a legend.**

Getting started

1 Have you heard of the legend of Sinbad the sailor and his adventures?
He likes helping people and gives all of his money away.

2 What else can you find out about Sinbad?
Do you know any of his stories?

1 Read the beginning of this story.
   It is the start of one of Sinbad's adventures.

Sinbad and the Roc

Once upon a time, there was a man called Sinbad. He loved to go to faraway lands and find treasure. Now you might think that Sinbad was rich. But he gave his treasure away to anyone who was poor.

One day, he found he had nothing left. Sinbad was not upset.

'I need to find more treasure,' he cried.

'It's time for another adventure!'

Sinbad went down to the seashore. He needed a big ship to sail to faraway lands. He found some sailors who wanted to go with him. The sailors packed the ship with plenty of food and plenty of water. Soon they were ready to leave.

At first, the sea was calm and the sun was shining. But soon a great storm blew up. The ship was tossed about on the waves. All of the food and water was washed into the sea. The sailors were very worried.

Sinbad was not worried. 'Cheer up, lads!' he said to the sailors. 'I can see an island up ahead. Maybe we can get food to eat and water to drink. Let's go and see what we can find.'

Sinbad rowed to the island. He started climbing a hill to look around the island. He didn't see the giant bird flying overhead. It had an enormous snake in its beak.

But the sailors had seen it! 'Help! It's a Roc!' one of the sailors yelled. 'It will kill us all!' The sailors were scared. They sailed away from the island as fast as they could.

Soon, Sinbad got to the top of the hill and looked around. He could see sticks – lots of sticks. This wasn't an island. This was a nest. And it wasn't a hill that he had climbed. It was the Roc's egg!

The sky above him began to grow darker …

Ian Whybrow

Answer the questions about the story.

a   Who is the main character of the story?

b   Why did Sinbad decide he needed to go on another adventure?

c   Where did Sinbad want to go?

d   Why did the food and water fall overboard?

e   Why did Sinbad row to the island?

f   What tells us that the Roc isn't an ordinary bird?

g   Do you think you would have been scared like the sailors?

h   Write three words that describe Sinbad's character.

> What did you do to try to find the answers to these questions?

2   How do we know *Sinbad and the Roc* in Activity 1 is a legend?

a   Does the story have a main character who is a hero or heroine?

b   What dangerous task, possibly involving a monster or a powerful enemy, happens in this story?

c   Do you think this story could possibly be true or is it an event linked to a culture or a set of beliefs?

3   Read the Language focus box.

Language focus

Some words use an apostrophe to show where a letter, or letters, have been missed out.

Example:

do n**o**t = don't   I **wi**ll = I'll

These words are called **contractions**.

The apostrophe takes the place of the missing letter or letters.

a Copy the contraction in each of these sentences.

b Now write out the two words it replaces.

- It's time for another adventure!

- Let's go and see what we can find.

- That's a Roc!

- This isn't an island.

> 4.10 Planning a legend

We are going to...

- **plan a legend.**

Getting started

1 Talk about the characters in the story *Sinbad and the Roc* in Session 4.9, Activity 1.

2 What do you know about them?

Sinbad the sailor   **The Roc**

1 With a partner, re-read the beginning of Sinbad's adventure *Sinbad and the Roc* in Session 4.9, Activity 1.

   a Discuss what might happen next.

   b What new characters might be introduced?

   c Does the Roc discover Sinbad?

   d How does Sinbad make it home?

   e Does Sinbad find any treasure to share with people once he gets home?

2 Now, on your own, make a storyboard of a new adventure about Sinbad the sailor.

   a Divide a piece of paper into six boxes. Write the story title in the first box and number the following boxes 1 to 5.

   b Draw a picture and/or write notes in each box to tell the story. Use each box to represent a new paragraph in the story.

Story title	1	2
3	4	5

3 On your storyboard write some adverbs or sentence openers you might use at the beginning of each paragraph of the story.

〉 4.11 Writing a legend

We are going to...

- **write a legend.**

Getting started

1 Discuss this recipe for how to write a legend.

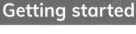

How to write a legend

You will need:

- a hero or heroine as the main character

- a dangerous task (sometimes involving a monster or a powerful enemy)

- an event in the past that is true or was possibly true, or an event linked to a culture or a set of beliefs.

What to do:

1 Explain when in history the legend is set.

2 Introduce the main character.

3 Explain how difficult and dangerous the task is.

4 Make the main character very brave.

5 Make sure the main character is successful.

2 Does the plan of your Sinbad adventure include all these things?

1 Look at the storyboard you made in Session 4.10, Activity 2.

Discuss what might happen next.

a Practise telling your legend to yourself.

- Use the words and phrases (including the adverbs) from the words you have written in your storyboard.

- Are you happy with the story for your legend?

- Do you need to make any changes to it?

b Practise telling your story to a partner.

How are we doing?

Does your partner have any suggestions to improve your legend?

2 Write your legend.

Include some dialogue. Use the Language focus box to help you.

Write a new paragraph for every picture in your storyboard.

Language focus

Dialogue is another term for speech in stories. When you write dialogue you:

- start a new speaker on a new line

- use speech marks around the words characters say.

Speech marks like this " show where the words a character says **begin**.

Speech marks like this " show where the words a character says **end**.

Sometimes, speech marks are shown like this: '...'

Phrases like he said are not included inside the speech marks.

Example: "Use speech marks like this," he said.

Remember, there are lots of different words you can use instead of said like asked, replied, shouted, muttered.

3   When you have finished writing your legend, read it aloud to check it.

Add in any little words you might have missed out.

› 4.12 Improving your legend

We are going to...

- **proofread our story.**

Getting started

Re-read the legend you wrote in the Session 4.11.

1   Proofread your writing. Find at least three things to improve.

- Does your legend make sense? Have you missed out any important ideas?

- Check your opening and ending. Are they right for this story?

- Check the vocabulary.
  Can you use more powerful or more descriptive words?

- Check your sentences. Have you used some good joining words?

- Check you haven't made any mistakes with your punctuation and spelling.

How did you work out how to write a word you weren't sure how to spell?

How am I doing?

What have you done well? What could you do better next time?

Write two statements about what you are pleased with in your legend.

Write one target for something you want to improve on.

Look what I can do!

- ☐ I can read and answer questions about myths and legends.
- ☐ I can identify and use pronouns appropriately.
- ☐ I can recognise and discuss the features of myths and legends.
- ☐ I can write paragraphs and understand how their openings establish links in a story.
- ☐ I can write multi-clause sentences using simple connectives of time, place and cause.
- ☐ I can plan, write and proofread a legend.

Check your progress

1 Copy the table.

Read the statements and tick (✓) which type of story they are true for. Some are true for more than one.

	Myths	Legends
The stories were told before they were written down.		
The stories are set in the past.		
The stories explain how or why something happens.		
The stories are about heroes or gods.		

2 Change these pairs of sentences into compound sentences by joining them with a connective. Replace some of the nouns and noun phrases in the sentences with pronouns.

Continued

a   The elephant lived in the jungle. The trees made the elephant unwell.

b   The cow was feeling hungry. The cow ate all the flowers in the park.

c   Does Stefan like cats? Does Stefan prefer dogs?

d   The teacher looked at the children. The children stopped talking.

e   The giant looked down at the people. The giant laughed.

Projects

Group project: Choose one of the legends you have written about Sinbad.

Decide who will play each character. Is a narrator needed?

Practise performing the legend.

Perform the legend to your class.

Pair project: Discuss the myth and legends you have read in this unit.

Which story did you enjoy the most?

Write three things you enjoyed about the story and then share your thoughts with your partner.

Did you both like the same story?

Did you both like the same things about the stories?

Solo project: Search in books or on the internet for a myth or legend. Write a review of the myth or legend you have read and share it with your partner or group.

5 ▸ Writing to each other

❯ 5.1 What do we write?

We are going to...

- **read and explore a range of written communication.**

Getting started

1 Have you ever received any mail?

2 Talk about the different types of mail you might get. Write a list.

3 When are you likely to get mail?

4 Who delivers your mail?

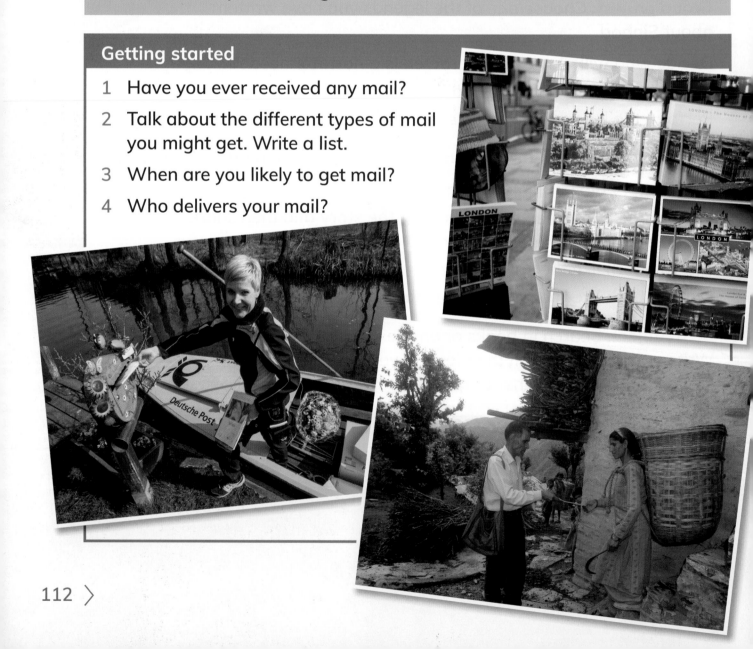

1 This unit is about Mrs Sabella, a teacher from Argentina, who goes to England to visit her sick mother. She stays with her sister and Arturo, her nephew.

Read these different texts. Then, answer these questions.

a Discuss which text is an email. How do you know?

b Discuss which text is a postcard. How do you know?

c Discuss which text is a letter. How do you know?

Text A

| From: artgarcia@zen.co.uk |
| To: Sonia.sabell@lemail.com |
| Date: 25th May at 16:23 |
| Subject: Thank you! |

Dear Aunty Sonia,

Thank you for the books you kindly gave me for my birthday. I was too excited after my party to read, but I am going to start a book tonight.

How did you know that Francesca Simon was my favourite fiction writer? I love reading about her characters and their adventures. They make me laugh so hard. Do you think I'm like Horrid Henry or Perfect Peter?

I am really interested in cars and the non-fiction book about cars is amazing. I really like the section on huge, powerful cars! When I grow up I want to drive a bright red, fast, powerful sports car. Thank you again.

Lots of love,
Arturo

Text B

Rivadavia Oeste 477
Piso 2
J5102DFI
San Juan Buenos Aires
Saturday 18 July

Dear Sir,

I am writing to complain about the fact that some letters that were posted from your area took over five weeks to reach me. A number of letters were written and posted on the same day. The first arrived within ten days of being posted, but the last of these letters took nearly four times as long.

These letters were very important to me for they were written by people I care about. I am away from my home at the moment so it is particularly important to me that I receive letters promptly.

I would be grateful for an explanation about why some of these letters took so long.

Yours faithfully,
Sonia Sabella

Text C

Dear Class 3,

Look at what I saw in England today! The sound of all those feet marching and stamping at the same time was so loud: even louder than the trumpets!
I love all those red uniforms and funny, fluffy hats. Luckily the sun shone for us. I'll have so much to tell you when I get back to Argentina.

From Mrs Sabella

TO

Class 3

School St Maria

Marcos Seatre

San Miguel

Buenos Aires

Argentina

2 Answer these questions.

a Which text is making a complaint?

b What is the complaint about?

c Who is the 'thank you' to?

d What is Arturo saying 'thank you' for?

e Have you ever written a postcard?

f Why do you think people enjoy receiving postcards?

> **Reading tip**
>
> Read each text carefully. Notice the difference in style of each text.

> 5.2 Scanning or reading?

We are going to...

- **scan** or read texts to locate information to answer questions.

Getting started

You can read in different ways.

1 In pairs, discuss two different types of writing that:

- can be scanned

- need to be read carefully.

> **Key word**
>
> scan: to look quickly to find specific information

1 The next page has a note that Class 3 found when they arrived at school one day.

Quickly scan the text to answer these questions. Write the answers in your notebook.

a Who wrote the text?

b Where is she going?

c Why is she going away?

> **Reading tip**
>
> You can scan a text quickly when you want to find a particular word or piece of information. When you scan a text, you don't read every word.
>
> You can **read** a text slowly and carefully when you need to make sure you understand it thoroughly.

Dear Class 3,

Yesterday, I had some very sad news. My mother is very ill. I have to go to England to see her. When I am there, I will stay with my sister and her family. The good thing is that I will get to see my nephew, Arturo, who is the same age as you.

The other bad news is that I may be away from Argentina for a few weeks. While I am away, Mrs Diaz will be your teacher. Please work hard for her and show her what wonderful children you are and how much you have learnt so far this year.

I will write to you from England and tell you what I am doing.

I hope you will write to me too. I will miss you all.

From,
Mrs Sabella

2   Now read the text slowly and carefully to find the answers to these questions. Write the answers in your notebook.

   a   Who will the writer be staying with?

   b   Who is Arturo?

   c   What does the writer ask the children to do while she is away?

   d   Does the writer like Class 3? How do you know?

3   Share your answers to Activities 1 and 2 with a partner. Talk about the difference between scanning and reading carefully.

> **Reading tip**
>
> When you scan a piece of writing, look for key words to provide you with basic information.

Language focus

Prepositions are words that show the relationship between a noun (or pronoun) with another word in the sentence. They often can show the 'position' of something.

Example: My mother, who lives **in** England, is very ill.

I will stay **with** my sister and her family.

I will write to you **from** England.

Key word

preposition: a word that shows the relationship between a noun with another word in the sentence

4   Mrs Sabella used some prepositions in her letter.

Use each of these prepositions in sentences of your own.

under   near   around

> 5.3 Looking at synonyms

We are going to...

* **explore and use synonyms.**

Getting started

With a partner, list as many different words you can think of that you could use instead of the words *happy* and *sad*.

1   Read Mrs Sabella's letter and talk about what she says.

* What happened?
* Who was there?
* When did it happen?
* Where did it happen?
* Why or how did it happen?

28 River Avenue,
Reading,
Berkshire,
RG9 5SN,
United Kingdom.
Saturday 17 May

Dear Class 3,

Yesterday, my sister looked after my mother for the day, so Arturo and I went for a day out in London. We had a very enjoyable time.

First, we went to see Buckingham Palace, where Queen Elizabeth lives. It's a huge house. Arturo and I counted 68 windows! Why do you imagine the Queen and her husband need that many rooms?

After leaving the palace, we strolled in the sun beside the River Thames. It's a very wide river and it's extremely busy with ships, speedboats, water taxis and water buses. There are even river police!

Then we went to Westminster and saw the Houses of Parliament. This is where the **government** makes the laws in the UK. The Houses of Parliament are next to the Thames.

Finally, we went across Westminster Bridge for a ride on the London Eye. This was Arturo's favourite part of the day! The London Eye is a massive wheel. You've probably seen it on TV because they set off fireworks from the London Eye for important celebrations. You can see some excellent views of London from the top.

I hope you are working hard and learning lots of things. I miss you all.

From,
Mrs Sabella

Glossary

government: a group of people who are given the power to run a country

How did you decide whether to scan or read the text carefully when answering the questions? Why?

2 Write the answers to these questions.

a List three things that Mrs Sabella and Arturo saw.

b What did Mrs Sabella find surprising about Buckingham Palace?

c Why are the Houses of Parliament important to the UK?

d   When is the London Eye on TV?

e   How do we know Mrs Sabella went on the London Eye?

3   Mrs Sabella used some interesting words in her letter.
Can you find some of the interesting words she used?
Why do you think she used them?

Language focus

Synonyms are words that have similar meanings.

Example: *cheerful* is a synonym of *happy*;

miserable is a synonym of *sad.*

Using synonyms for ordinary words can make your writing
more interesting and precise.

---

a   Copy the table into your notebook.

b   Beside each word, write a word or words from the
box that have the same meaning.

amazing   house   huge   imagine   massive   wide

fun   palace   beautiful   speedboat   strolled   water taxi

Ordinary words	Synonyms
big	
nice	
walked	
building	
boat	
think	

c   Add one more synonym for each ordinary word in the table.

› 5.4 What does a letter look like?

We are going to...

- **explore and recognise the layout of a letter.**

Getting started

Look at the letters in Session 5.1 and Session 5.3. Discuss:

1 what is similar about them

2 what is different about them

3 how a letter written in England gets to a school in Argentina.

Language focus

When you write a **letter**, you need to include five things:

1 **heading** – including the address of the person who is writing the letter and the date

2 **greeting** – who the letter is to

3 **body** – the information in the letter

4 **ending** – shows the letter has ended

5 **signature** – the name of the person who wrote the letter.

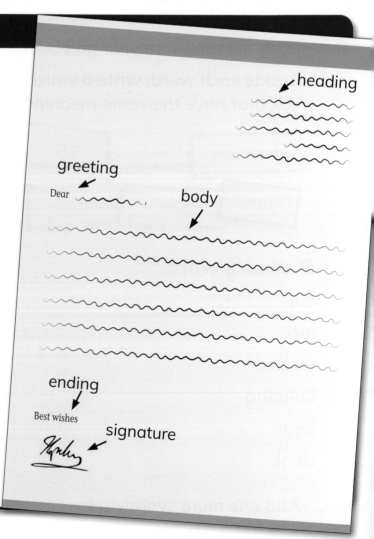

1 In pairs look at the letter from Mrs Sabella to Class 3
in Session 5.3 Activity 1.

In the letter, find:

- the heading
- the greeting
- the body
- the ending
- the signature

2 Now you are going to write a letter to Mrs Sabella's nephew, introducing yourself.

Firstly, write a plan in your notebook. Explain:

- who you are
- what you look like
- what you enjoy doing in your spare time
- who is in your family.

3 Write your letter. Remember to use the correct layout.

Make sure you write the information in the body of your letter in a sensible order.

Look at the Language focus box in Activity 1 if you need help.

Remember to use interesting words!

How are we doing?

Share your letter with a partner.

Ask them to check the layout is correct.

Is there anything you can improve?

What did they like about your letter?

> 5.5 Looking at homophones

We are going to...

- **recognise and write homophones.**

Getting started

1 Can you remember what information we need to include in a party invitation?

2 Write an invitation to a friend asking them to your party.

3 Have you included all the important information?
Look back at Unit 2 to check your invitation.

1 Read Mrs Sabella's latest letter on the next page.

a What has been happening in England?

b Write answers to these questions in your notebook.
Decide if you need to scan for information or to read carefully.

- What sort of letter did Arturo send to his aunt, Mrs Sabella?

- Where was Arturo's birthday party held?

- What happened at the party?

28 River Avenue
Reading,
Berkshire
RG9 5SN
United Kingdom
Sunday 25 May

Dear Class 3,

Can you guess what's happening here?
Here's my party invitation from Arturo.
The party was very exciting. A **gaucho** came and
showed us how to do tricks with a lasso. It was
more difficult than it looked! Arturo thought it
was great fun.

I'll write a proper letter soon.

From,
Mrs Sabella

2   Remember, most nouns have
    singular and **plural** forms.

Arturo
would like to invite
Aunty Sonia
to his 8th birthday party
on 24 May
from 4:30 to 6:00
at the Town Hall
RSVP

Key words

singular: one single thing. For
example, book is a singular
noun

plural: more than one thing.
For example, books is a plural
noun. For most regular nouns,
the plural form is made
by adding –s or –es. Some
irregular nouns have different
plural forms

Glossary

gaucho: an
Argentinian cowboy

a Copy and fill in this table in your notebook.

Singular	Plural
birthday	birthdays
trick	
balloon	
cake	

b What happens when a singular noun ends in –x, –sh, –s or –ch? Copy and fill in this table in your notebook.

Singular	Plural
box	boxes
class	
brush	
bench	

c Some nouns have **irregular plural forms**.
Copy this table in your notebook.
Fill it in with the plural nouns in the boxes.

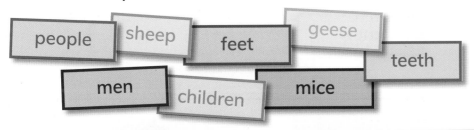

people   sheep   feet   geese   teeth   men   children   mice

Singular	Plural		Singular	Plural
child	children		sheep	
mouse			goose	
person			foot	
tooth			man	

3   Look at these lines from Mrs Sabella's letter.
    Do you know what the words in bold have in common?
    Read the Language focus box. Are you correct?

> **Dear** Class 3,
>
> Can you guess what's happening **here**?
> I'll **write** a proper letter soon.

Language focus

A homophone is a word that sounds the same as another word
but has a different meaning and spelling.
Example:

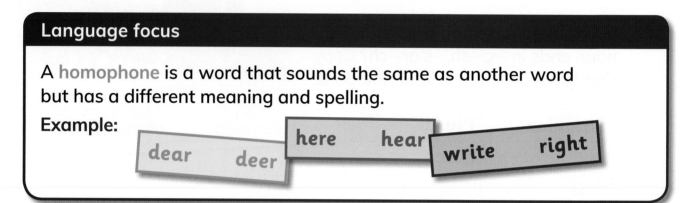

a   Write the two different meanings of each of these homophones.

b   Write a homophone that matches each of these words.

knew   passed   daze

126

> 5.6 A letter of complaint

We are going to...

- **discuss letters of complaint.**

Getting started

1 Discuss when you think we use formal letters and when you think we use informal letters.

2 List as many different situations you can think of when you could write a letter.

3 Now organise these types of letters into formal and informal letters.

1 Read this letter written by Mrs Sabella in Session 5.1.
   Discuss the questions in a group.

   a How do you know this is a letter of complaint?

   b How is the letter of complaint different from Mrs Sabella's other letters?

   c How is this letter the same as other letters Mrs Sabella has written?

   d Is this letter a formal or informal letter?

Rivadavia Oeste 477
Piso 2
J5102DFI
San Juan,
Buenos Aires
Saturday 18 July

Dear Sir,

I am writing to complain about the fact that some letters that were posted from your area took over five weeks to reach me. A number of letters were written and posted on the same day. The first arrived within ten days of being posted, but the last of these letters took nearly four times as long.

These letters were very important to me for they were written by people I care about. I am away from my home at the moment so it is particularly important to me that I receive letters promptly.

I would be grateful for an explanation about why some of these letters took so long.

Yours faithfully,
Sonia Sabella

---

2   Discuss the answers to these questions with a partner.

   a   When do you think we need to write a letter of complaint?

   b   What are the important things that need to be included in the body of a letter of complaint?

   c   Should a letter of complaint be written in a formal or informal way? Why?

> ### Writing tip
>
> When you write a letter of complaint think about:
>
> - why you are writing
> - what evidence you have
> - how the situation has made you feel
> - what you would like to happen.
>
> Use powerful words to explain your complaint, but never be rude.

3   Can you find any multi-clause sentences in Mrs Sabella's letter of complaint? Which connectives did she use?

Look back at Session 4.6 to remind yourself about multi-clause sentences and connectives.

› 5.7 Beginning and ending letters

We are going to...

- **explore how letters begin and end.**

Getting started

Look at some formal and informal letters.

What do they all have in common?

1 Different letters need different greetings.

   a Copy the table. Sort these greetings into ones you would use for formal and informal letters.

Dear Sir   To Mr Henderson   Greetings   Dear Cindy   Dear Mrs Trainor

Hi Tuhil   Good morning   To the manager

Dear Aunty Su   Dear Madam   Hello Jake

Formal greetings	Informal greetings

   b What do you notice about the informal greetings?

2 Discuss how letters end.
   Look at some examples.

   a Write five letter endings
      you might use if you were
      writing an informal letter.

   b Discuss which letter
      ending you think is used
      the most for:

      > formal letters

      > informal letters

Writing tip

These letter endings can be used for formal letters:

> Yours sincerely
> Yours faithfully

If you know the name of the person you are writing to, end the letter with *Yours sincerely*.

If you don't know the name of the person you are writing to, for example when you use *Dear Sir* or *Dear Madam* at the start, end the letter with *Yours faithfully*.

> 5.8 Looking at sentences in a letter

We are going to...

- **explore, understand and use different types of sentences.**

Getting started

1 Write an example of a statement.
2 Write an example of an exclamation.
3 Write an example of a question.

1 Read the letter on the next page from Mrs Sabella.
   Answer the questions in your notebook.

   a Why has Mrs Sabella not written for a while?

   b Why do you think Mrs Sabella is not living with her sister
      and Arturo any more?

c What has the weather been like in England?

d Do you think how Mrs Sabella's class behaves matters to her?

e Why do you think Mrs Sabella wrote this letter?

8 Tree Lane
Caversham
Reading,
Berkshire
RG47 6TB
United Kingdom
Tuesday 16 June

Dear Class 3,

It's been a long time since I last wrote to you because my mother was in hospital for a few weeks. She had an operation last week and now she's getting better. That's good news, isn't it? I have now left my sister's house and I am staying with my mother at her house. I will stay with my mother until she is completely better.

I was able to spend some time with Arturo last week. It was raining, so we had to stay inside. The weather has been terrible! We spent an afternoon drawing pictures of things we have seen. I think Arturo's pictures were better than mine.

When I know that my mother is really better, I'll book my ticket back to Argentina. Are you all behaving well and working hard?

From,
Mrs Sabella

2 Look back at Mrs Sabella's letter in Activity 1.

a Copy an example of a statement.
Write a sentence explaining when we use statements.

b Copy an example of an exclamation.
Write a sentence explaining when we use exclamations.

c Copy an example of a question.
Write a sentence explaining when we use questions.

3 Read these sentences.

- We draw pictures all afternoon before we ate tea.
- Do you enjoyed drawing pictures too?
- Watch out, I'll soon be back to made you work hard!
- I'll came home as soon as I can.

a What is wrong with each of the sentences?

b Copy the sentences. <u>Underline</u> the verbs in each sentence.

c Write out the sentences correctly. What do you notice?

How did you decide on the tense for each verb
to make the sentences correct?

> 5.9 Other written communication

We are going to...

- **explore key features of emails and SMS messages.**

Getting started

1 What is an email?

2 What is a SMS message?

3 Discuss with a partner how you think these are different from letters. Why?

1 Read these two messages from Mrs Sabella.
  Did these messages come by post?
  How do you know?

  a Are there any verbs in the email?
    Are there any verbs in the SMS message?

  b Are there any pronouns in the email?
    Are there any pronouns in the SMS message?

  c Are there sentences in the email?
    Are there any sentences in the SMS message?

> **Key words**
>
> **verb:** word that tells you what someone or something does
>
> **pronoun:** word that replaces nouns and noun phrases

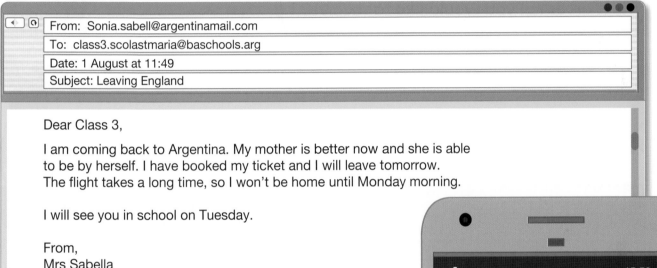

From: Sonia.sabell@argentinamail.com
To: class3.scolastmaria@baschools.arg
Date: 1 August at 11:49
Subject: Leaving England

Dear Class 3,

I am coming back to Argentina. My mother is better now and she is able to be by herself. I have booked my ticket and I will leave tomorrow. The flight takes a long time, so I won't be home until Monday morning.

I will see you in school on Tuesday.

From,
Mrs Sabella

2 Change the SMS message into proper sentences. Write the message in sentences in your notebook.

  a <u>Underline</u> the verbs in your sentences.

  b Circle the pronouns.

all 15:58 🔋

Sonia   02–Aug 15:55

Hi Class 3,

At the airport. Home at last ☺
See you tomorrow.
Mrs Sabella

34

3 Listen carefully to this conversation between Aunty Sonia and Arturo.

Write an email from Arturo to Pedro in Class 3. Remember, Arturo would have to introduce himself and ask Pedro some questions.

How am I doing?

Read your email to Pedro.
Is it written in the style of an email?
Is it an email you would like to receive?

> Remember, Arturo's Aunty Sonia is Mrs Sabella.

> ## 5.10 Talking about mail

We are going to...

- **discuss a letter received.**

Getting started

Talk with a partner about what mail you have received.

1 How did you feel when you read the mail?

2 Did you keep the mail?

3 Did you show your mail to anyone else?

4 Did you write back?

> Did you know that every year the American mail service delivers about 142 billion pieces of mail – that's 142,000,000,000 items!

1 In pairs make a mind map to show different sorts of mail and the different reasons for writing them.

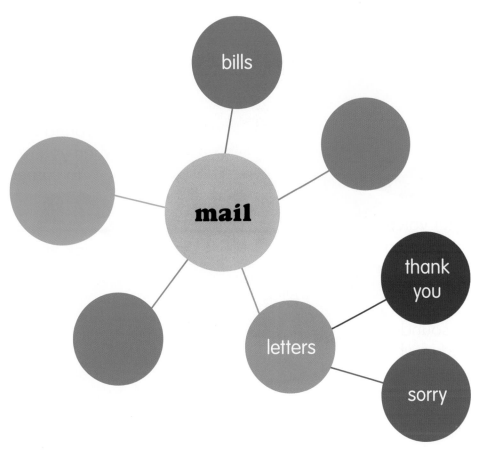

2 Talk with a partner about a time when you got some mail. (It can be fiction or a true story.)

- Read all the speech bubbles in **1 d** about speaking and listening.

- Decide who will be the speaker and the listener.

- **Speaker:** practise telling your partner your mail story.

- **Speaker and listener:** tell each other whether you followed the tips in the speech bubbles.

Speaker

Listener

The way that you talk is as important as what you say.

When you listen, the way you sit or stand can help the speaker.

Look at the people you are talking to.

Don't move around too much when you're listening to someone.

Make your voice sound interesting.

Look at the person who is talking to you.

Try to sound interested in what you are saying.

Try to look interested in what the person is talking to you about.

3   With a partner, discuss why more emails and SMS messages are now sent instead of handwritten letters.

4   In a group, practise telling the story of Mrs Sabella's trip to England. Use the letters in this unit to help you.

Reading tip

Read Mrs Sabella's letters in order, starting with those in Session 5.2. This will help you understand the order in which things have happened.

> 5.11 Writing a letter

We are going to...

- **plan and write a letter.**

Getting started

1 Explain to a partner what the past tense is.

Do they agree with you?

2 With a partner, say the past tense of each of these verbs.

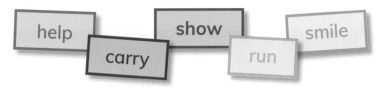

help
carry
show
run
smile

3 Why should you write most of your letter in the past tense?

1 You are going to write a letter to Mrs Sabella, telling her about what you have been doing during the time she has been away in England.

a With a partner, discuss things that you can include in your letter.

How are we doing?

Listen carefully to your partner's ideas. If they have an idea that you think would be really good to include in a letter to Mrs Sabella, tell them why you like it.

2 Make notes in your notebook to plan your letter. Think about:

    a how you can organise your ideas into paragraphs, making sure the information in the body of your letter is written in a sensible order

    b the vocabulary you use, including powerful words to describe what you have done

    c your sentences, including multi-clause sentences using connectives.

3 Write your letter to Mrs Sabella.

    Remember to write your letter using the correct layout.

> 5.12 Improving your letter

We are going to...

- **proofread for grammar, spelling and punctuation errors.**

Getting started

1 Can you remember the five things you need to include in the layout of a letter? Try not to look back in this book to check!

2 Have you included all five things in your letter?

1 Re-read your letter. Is your reason for writing clear? Could you:

    a organise your ideas more clearly?

    b join simple sentences into multi-clause sentences using connectives?

    c use more interesting vocabulary?

2 Check your letter carefully.

    a Are there any mistakes in your writing?

    b Have you missed out any words?

    c Have you used the past tense when you needed to?

Listening tip

Read your letter aloud to yourself. If you listen carefully, mistakes you have made will be more obvious.

d Is the punctuation correct?
Look at the Language focus box to help you.

Language focus

Punctuation is important in your writing.

- Use a *capital letter* at the beginning of your sentences and for people's names and place names.

- End every sentence with a *full stop* (**.**), *a question mark* (**?**) or an *exclamation mark* (**!**).

- Use *commas* (**,**) to separate items in lists.

- Use an *apostrophe* (**'**) to show where you have joined two words together and shortened them.

---

3 Check that all the words in your letter are spelled correctly.
Make a note of any words you found difficult to spell.
Use a dictionary to check them.

Which strategies did you use to check your spelling?
Which were the most useful strategies?

4 Write your final letter neatly.

How am I doing?

Can you write quickly and neatly, with joined handwriting?

Are your letters the same size?

Are **b, d, f, h, k, l** and **t** taller and do **f, g, j, p, q,** and **y** have tails below the line?

Have you got even spaces between the letters and the words?

Look what I can do!

- ☐ I can read and explore a range of written communication.
- ☐ I can scan/read texts to locate relevant information to answer questions.
- ☐ I can recognise and write synonyms and homophones.
- ☐ I can understand and use different types of sentences and their grammar appropriately.
- ☐ I can plan and write a letter.
- ☐ I can proofread for grammar, spelling and punctuation errors.

Check your progress

1 Are the following statements true or false?

a You only write letters to people you like.

b Letters can be about anything.

c Letters always begin with the word *Dear*.

2 Copy these sentences. Add the punctuation marks and capital letters.

a mrs sabella wrote to her class while she was in england

b did you count how many letters she wrote

c were going to miss her letters when she comes home said sita

3 Find the synonyms. Match the words in the yellow circle with the more interesting words in the blue circle. Then write the pairs of words.

big

little

good

bad

nice

tiny

pleasant

wonderful

enormous

terrible

Continued

4 Add a preposition to each sentence.

   a The guards walked _____ the gates at Buckingham Palace.

   b Mrs Sabella did a tour of London _____ a bus.

5 Write a homophone for each of these words.

   a right   **b** two   **c** rein   **d** by

Projects

Group project: Talk about something in your school that could be improved. Each write a letter to your headteacher explaining what you would like to see improved in the school and why.

Choose the best letter from the group to send to them and then wait for a reply.

Pair project: Have an email conversation with a friend or member of your family.

Write about what you have learnt at school this week and remember to write questions for them to answer in response.

Solo project: Think of the most amazing present you would love to receive and then write a letter thanking a real or imaginary person for it.

Remember to explain why the present is so special to you and what you plan to do with it.

6 Bringing stories alive

> 6.1 Reading a playscript

We are going to...

- **read a playscript and answer questions about it.**

Getting started

Discuss these questions with a partner.

1. What is a play?
2. Have you ever seen a play?
3. Have you ever acted in a play?
4. Where are plays often watched?

1 Read the beginning of this play by Lynne Rickards.

Four Clever Brothers, Part 1

Characters

Judge – the narrator and wise man

Gilad – a foolish man

The four brothers:

Tazim – the eldest brother, a natural leader, his brothers look up to him

Kamran – a hard worker

Sadiq – a serious young man

Latif – the youngest brother

> **Key word**
>
> **narrator:** the storyteller in a playscript

Stage directions

Four brothers walking along a path between two villages. The path is dry and sandy, with grass growing on each side. As they walk, the brothers speak softly to each other. Judge is standing to the side of the stage.

Judge: I am Adil the **judge**. I am going to tell you a story. It takes place in a dry and dusty desert land.

My story concerns Gilad, the camel owner, who came to me one hot afternoon to settle an argument. This was an unusual case, and I remember it well. Everything I will tell you is true.

There once were four brothers, who were very good hunters. Their father taught them how to track an animal by listening and looking for clues on the ground.

Tazim:	Do you see footprints on this path? Look, just here.
Kamran:	It looks like something has passed this way recently.
Sadiq:	They are smaller than the prints of a horse's hoof.
Latif:	But they are spaced well apart. I would say it was a camel.
Tazim:	Yes, that's just what I was thinking.
	Suddenly, a man rushes towards the four brothers, waving his arms in distress.
Gilad:	Help! You, there! Please help me. Have you seen my camel? I'm sure someone has stolen it!
Judge:	The four brothers looked at each other with worried faces. Then they looked at the camel owner.

Glossary

judge: someone who decides who or what is right or wrong in an argument

2   Re-read the playscript in Activity 1. Answer the questions about it.

> **Reading tip**
>
> Often, when you read something for the first time, you get an idea of what happens. The second time you read it, you think more about the details.

  a   How many actors are there in this play?

  b   Who is the eldest and who is the youngest of the brothers?

  c   Where is the story set?

  d   What were the four brothers good at?

  e   How do the brothers know a camel has recently passed by?

  f   Why did the four brothers look at each other with worried faces?

3 Answer these questions about the characters in the playscript in Activity 1.

   a What is the job of a narrator in a play?

   b What are your first impressions of the character Gilad?

   c Write three words that describe how the brothers might have felt when they first saw Gilad.

   d What questions would you have asked Gilad when you first met him?

   e The judge says his role is to settle arguments.
Can you think what the argument is going to be about?

4 Look again at the playscript in Activity 1.
Compare it to an ordinary story. Copy and complete the table.

Playscripts and stories	
Similarities	Differences

> 6.2 Looking closely at a playscript

We are going to...

- **discuss the layout of a playscript.**

Getting started

1 With a partner, write a list of different fiction and non-fiction texts, for example, poems and newspaper reports.

2 Talk about how each of them is laid out.

3 Do they use paragraphs, lists, bullet points, columns?

1 Look again at the beginning of *Four Clever Brothers* in Session 6.1 Activity 1.

Language focus

A **playscript** needs:

- a title, for example: *Four Clever Brothers*
- a list of characters, for example: **Judge** – *the narrator and wise man*
- stage directions, for example: *Four brothers walking along a path ...*
- dialogue, for example: **Tazim:** *Do you see footprints on this path?*

Write the answers to these questions.

a   What do you read first in a playscript?

b   Why is it helpful to have a list of characters?

c   What are stage directions and why are they important?

d   How is dialogue written?

Four Clever Brothers

Characters

> **Judge** – the narrator and wise man

> **Gilad** – a foolish man

> The four brothers:

> **Tazim** – the eldest brother, a natural leader, his brothers look up to him

> **Kamran** – a hard worker

> **Sadiq** – a serious young man

> **Latif** – youngest brother

Stage directions *Four brothers walking along a path between two villages. The path is dry and sandy, with grass growing on each side. As they walk, the brothers speak softly to each other. Judge standing to the side of the stage.*

Dialogue

Judge: I am Adil the judge. I am going to tell you a story.
It takes place in a dry and dusty desert land.

Key word

stage directions: instructions in a play that help guide the actors or give details about scenery, etc.

---

147 >

2 Read what happens next.

Four Clever Brothers, Part 2

Tazim: We would like to help you, sir.
Tell me, is your camel blind in one eye?

Gilad: Yes, it is!

Kamran: And is it **lame** in one foot?

Gilad: Yes, that is true too! It is an old camel, and a bad-tempered beast, but it's the only one I've got.

Sadiq: I'm sure we can help you find it.

Latif: Tracking animals is what we do best.

Gilad: *(to himself)* I am very pleased that the brothers seem to know my camel so well. But I wonder how that is possible.

Sadiq: I have another question for you, sir.
Was your camel carrying a sack of wheat on one side?

Gilad: Indeed it was.

Latif: And did it have a jar of honey on the other side?

Gilad: That is exactly right! Come, come, you must think I am a fool. How do you know so much about my camel? You four men must have stolen my camel?

Write answers to these questions.

a How do we know when a character speaks?

b Which brother:

- tells Gilad that they can help find the camel
- asks if the camel was carrying wheat
- asks if the camel was carrying honey?

> **Glossary**
>
> **lame:** unable to walk normally

c How many questions do the brothers ask Gilad?

d Why is (to himself) in italics?

3 With a partner, discuss why you think playscripts are laid out in the way that they are.

> **Listening tip**
>
> Take turns to listen to each other's ideas and suggestions. Think about and respond to what your partner says.

> 6.3 Writing dialogue and performing a play

We are going to...

- **write dialogue in a playscript and perform a play.**

Getting started

1 Discuss with a partner what 'dialogue' is.

2 Look for examples of dialogue in your reading books.

3 How do you know which words are spoken by a character in a story?

4 How do you know which words are spoken by a character in a playscript?

1 Look at this cartoon.

a Write the words spoken by the characters in this cartoon using speech marks and dialogue words.

> Can I act the part of the judge?

> Which character do you want to act?

> That is a great idea.

> I'd like to be Gilad.

Writing tip

Remember, when you write dialogue you:

- start a new speaker on a new line
- only use speech marks around the words characters say.

b Now write the cartoon in the form of a playscript.

2 Read the next part of the play. It has been written as a paragraph in a story. Rewrite the story as a playscript. Think carefully about how you are going to lay it out.

> Think carefully about how dialogue is laid out in a playscript.

Example:

Character	**Dialogue**
Tazim:	No sir, we have not stolen your camel! Do we look like camel thieves?

Remember, dialogue in a playscript is written without speech marks.

Glossary

arrested: to be taken away by people

Four Clever Brothers, Part 3

'No sir, we have not stolen your camel! Do we look like camel thieves?' exclaimed Tazim. 'We have simply been walking along this path. I think you must have lost your camel somewhere else,' suggested Kamran.

'How could we have stolen it? A camel is too big to hide in a pocket! Feel free to search for yourself,' laughed Sadiq.

'Believe us, sir. We have never even seen your camel!' explained Latif.

Tazim went on to explain, 'We have simply worked out what your camel is like from the many clues it left behind.'

'What rubbish! I will have you **arrested!**' shouted Gilad.

Lynne Rickards

How am I doing?

Can the paragraph now be read as a playscript?
Have you included stage directions?

3   In a group of six, act *Four Clever Brothers* so far.

a   Decide who will play each character.

b   Read through the play script as a group.

c   Discuss how each character will act.

When you act a character, think about how you move and react to the other characters on the stage.

d   Discuss the movements of each character.

e   Act the play so far.

How do you use the information in a playscript to act a character?

> ## 6.4 What happens next?

We are going to...

- discuss what happens next in the play.

Getting started

With a partner answer these questions about the details of *Four Clever Brothers*.

1   What is the title of the play?

2   Where is the play set?

3   Who are the main characters in the play?

1 Write four sentences describing what has happened in the story so far.

Writing tip

Make notes about what has happened in the playscript so far. Use your notes to pick out the main events and then write the sentences.

2 Your teacher will read out a section of the playscript first, and then you will hear a recording of the same section read again. Listen carefully to both readings.

a With a partner discuss the differences between the two readings of the playscripts.

b Which reading did you enjoy listening to? Why?

c Look back at the text in Session 6.3 Activity 2. How do the question and exclamation marks tell you how to read the text?

3 Read the Language focus box.

Language focus

Often the c in a word sounds like a c. This is called a **hard c**.

Sometimes the c in a word can sound like an s. This is called a **soft c**.

Example: Latif: *Believe us, sir. We have never even seen your* **camel**. *We are* **innocent**!

camel = c as in cat (hard c)

inno**c**ent = c as in nice (soft c)

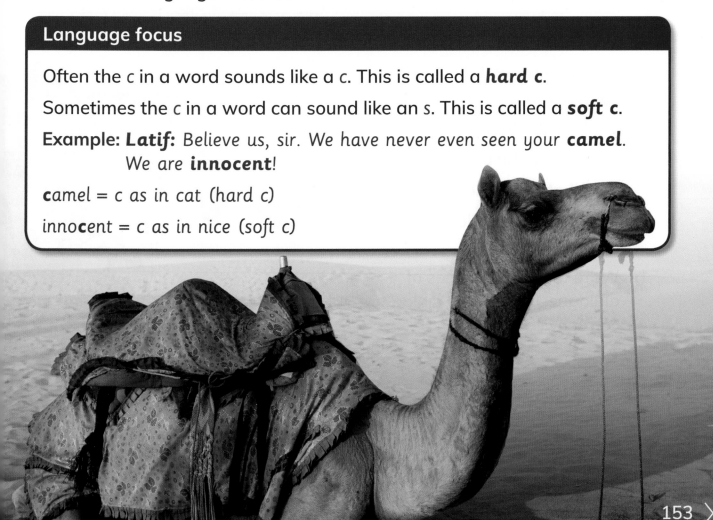

a   Copy the table. Sort the words from the playscript into the table.

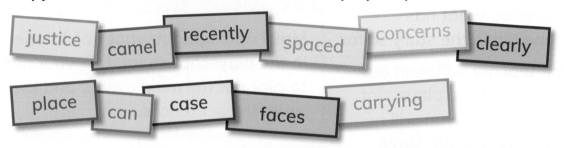

justice   camel   recently   spaced   concerns   clearly

place   can   case   faces   carrying

Soft c words (c sounds like 's')	Hard c words (c sounds like 'c')
	camel

b   What do you notice about the word *concerns*?

4   What happens next?

a   With a partner, discuss what you think might happen next.

- How do the brothers react?

- What does Gilad do?

- Where does Gilad take the brothers?

b   Write the next five lines of dialogue. Lay out the dialogue correctly.

Writing tip

Remember to include clear punctuation in your playscripts to help actors know how to read the words with the correct expression.

〉 6.5 Writing a playscript

We are going to...

- **plan and write a playscript.**

Getting started

1 In a small group, list as many traditional stories as you can.

2 Choose your favourite traditional story.

3 Explain to the group what you like about it.

1 Think of a traditional story you would like to write as a short playscript. You can write the whole story or write a part of it. You could change the story if you like. Plan your playscript by writing notes in your notebook.

a What are the key events in your play?

b Where will you set your play? List a few details about the setting.

c List the characters.

d Think about the stage directions that will help the actors. What stage directions will the characters need at the beginning of the play?

e Choose a title for your play.

2   Now write your playscript.
    Remember how a playscript is laid out:

Title: _____

Characters: _____

_____

Stage directions: _____

_____

_____

Character	Dialogue

What did you find most challenging about writing the playscript? Why?

❯ 6.6 Improving a playscript

We are going to...

- **improve and perform our playscript.**

Getting started

1   Read through your playscript.

2   Does it closely follow the traditional story you chose, or did you change the story?

3   Do you think others will enjoy watching the play you have written?

1 Proofread your playscript.
   Have you:

   a written a title?

   b written a list of characters?

   c written some stage directions?

   d laid out the dialogue correctly?

   e used punctuation clearly?

   f checked you have spelled words correctly?

> Remember, others need to be able to read what you have written so use your best handwriting.

2 Look at the vocabulary you have used.
   Can you change at least three words to more interesting synonyms or noun phrases?

3 Write or type a final copy of your playscript, improving and correcting any mistakes.

4 In a group, read through the playscript.

Speaking tip

Try to speak clearly in front of others.
Use different tones and expression in your voice to reflect your character and their emotions.

How are we doing?

Discuss what you think is good about each other's playscripts.
Is there anything that can be improved?
Do you think the playscript would work if a group acted it? Why?

Look what I can do!

- [ ] I can read and answer questions about a playscript.
- [ ] I can discuss the layout of a playscript.
- [ ] I can write dialogue in a playscript and perform a play.
- [ ] I can discuss what happens next in a play.
- [ ] I can plan and write a playscript.
- [ ] I can improve my playscript.

Check your progress

Answer these questions in your notebook.

1. List the four main things you need to include in the layout of a playscript.

2. Copy the sentences that are true.

   a. Playscripts don't use speech marks.

   b. Stories have stage directions.

   c. Playscripts have the dialogue next to the name of each character.

   d. Playscripts don't list characters.

   e. Stories are written using paragraphs.

3. Why is the use of punctuation important in a playscript?

4. Why are stage directions important in a playscript?

5. What do you need to remember when acting in a play?

Projects

Group project: Choose a traditional tale playscript and act it to the rest of the class.

- Remember to practise so you know your lines.
- Choose costumes for the characters.
- Think about the stage and where furniture might be needed.
- Rehearse before you perform.

Pair project: Imagine you are going to perform *Four Clever Brothers* to an audience of other learners and families. With a partner, list and describe or draw any scenery or props (items) you might need in the play.

Solo project: Choose a character in your play. Clearly describe the character so anyone acting that character will know how they should act him or her.

What does the character look like? What does the character wear? Does the character get on with the other characters? How should the character speak? How does the character change through the play?

7 Going on an adventure

> 7.1 Reading an adventure

We are going to...

- answer questions about an adventure story.

Getting started

1 What is an adventure?

2 Look at these photos.
What are the children doing?

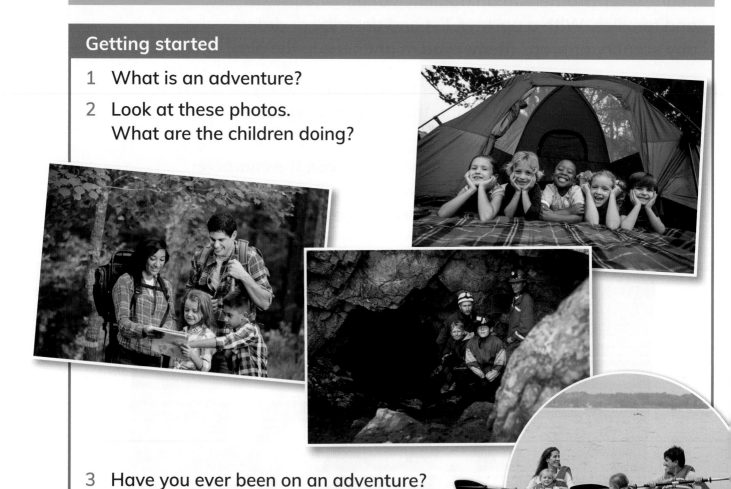

3 Have you ever been on an adventure?
4 Explain to a partner what happened.
5 Was it exciting or scary?

1 Listen as your teacher reads this playscript. Then read the story yourself. Read it in a dull boring voice, then use a more interesting voice.

A Day Out

Lucas, Fernando and Ana are on a day out with their parents in the rainforest. They are at the pool they normally swim in. Their parents are chatting to some friends they have met.

Fernando: This is no good. There are too many people here.

Lucas: I expect they're from the coach we saw in the car park.

Ana: Let's go up the river and see if there's another pool for us.

Lucas: Wander off? Mum and Dad won't like that.

Fernando: No, they wouldn't! There are snakes and spiders! We might fall into the river, or trip over a branch, or get stung, or bitten. Anyway, we might get lost.

Ana: OK. You stay here with all these people. I'm going by myself!

Ana starts to walk off. Lucas and Fernando look at each other.

Lucas: Ana, come back! What shall we do, Fernando? We can't let her go by herself. We'd better go after her. Come on!

Fernando: I don't like this! What will happen to us?

Reading tip

Look for the punctuation marks – they will help you understand the text and read with expression.

- Full stops mark the end of the sentence. You usually pause slightly between sentences.

- Question marks show you the end of the questions. What does your voice do when you ask a question?

- Exclamation marks show a sentence that must be read with expression. Match the expression to the meaning of the words. Is the character surprised? Excited? Bored? Worried? Determined? Angry?

- Commas are used to separate things in lists and to show which words go together in different sections of the sentence.

2   Answer these questions in your notebook.

  a   What are the names of the characters in the playscript?

  b   Why are the children cross?

  c   Why doesn't Lucas want to go further up the river?

  d   What is Fernando worried about?

  e   Write a sentence to describe the kind of person Ana is.

  f   Could this be the start of an adventure? Why?

  g   What would you have done in the same situation?

3   List all the contractions in the playscript.

Then write the two words each contraction is made from.

4   Act the playscript in groups. Then discuss in your group what might happen next. You could try acting your ideas.

> Remember, a contraction is a word with an apostrophe that shows where a letter, or letters, have been missed out. **Example:** *they're = they are*

› 7.2 Story beginnings

We are going to...

- **discuss story beginnings and explore the use of noun phrases.**

Getting started

1 Have you ever thought about how stories begin?

2 In pairs, take it in turns to read the first five lines of a fiction book to each other.

3 Which story beginning made you want to read more? Why?

1 Read these story beginnings.

Story beginning 1

My name is Alfie Small, and I'm a famous explorer. I have lots of dangerous adventures and always take my rucksack with me, just in case!

At the bottom of my garden, behind the **rickety** shed, is the special place I go exploring.

The grass grows long and the weeds are tall and I never know what I might find.

Today, I pushed through the weeds... and found a small boat floating on a small stream.

So I climbed aboard and paddled away.

Nick Ward

Glossary

rickety: likely to break

Story beginning 2

If you think this is the kind of story where five children, armed only with a bucket and spade, catch a dangerous band of **smugglers**, you'd be wrong. And if you think this is the kind of story where a poor helpless little girl is captured by a terrible gang of cut-throat pirates … you'd still be wrong, but a lot closer. Now, those are all the hints I'm going to give you. To find out what happens, you'd better read on …

Rose Impey

Glossary

smugglers: people who take things that aren't theirs from one place to another

Story beginning 3

Lily licked the mixing spoon like a large lollipop. She asked, 'Gran, why do they laugh at Granda sometimes?'

'Who laughs at your granda, my lovely?'

'People. They say he's strange.'

'Well, he is different from the rest, Lily,' said Gran. 'That's why I married him.'

Lily went out into the garden, through the gate and up the path to the hills. She found Granda sitting on a hump, whistling to himself.

'Granda, why do you like the hills so much?' asked Lily.

He smiled. 'Because these are Dragon Hills.'

'Real dragons?' asked Lily.

'Real sleeping dragons,' said Granda. 'Would you like to hear how I came to know all about them?'

Pippa Goodhart

2 Discuss the answers to these questions with a partner.

   a Which story beginning makes you want to read more of the story?

   b Which story do you think will be a good adventure story?

   c How do you know these are all fiction texts?

   d How do each of these story beginnings make you feel?

3 Copy these noun phrases into your notebook.

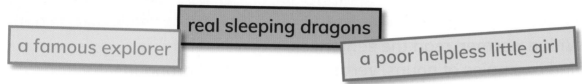

a famous explorer

real sleeping dragons

a poor helpless little girl

   a <u>Underline</u> the adjectives in each of the phrases.

   b (Circle) the nouns.

   c Are the adjectives before or after the nouns?

Remember, a **noun phrase** acts like a noun. Noun phrases always have a noun, and often also have adjectives to describe the noun.

When have you used noun phrases in your writing?
Why did you use them?

4 Now copy these sentences into your notebook.

   a <u>Underline</u> all the adjectives.

   b (Circle) all the nouns.

   c What do you notice about the position of the adjectives?

   d How are these sentences different from noun phrases?

The grass is long and the weeds are tall.

Dragons are long and scaly.

Pirates are scary and brave.

> 7.3 What happens next?

We are going to...

- **look at the language used in a passage and predict what might happen next.**

Getting started

1 With a partner, read the sentences.
2 Find examples of nouns, verbs, adjectives and pronouns.

> … I climbed aboard and paddled away. The stream got bigger and the water flowed faster, and soon I was racing along as fast as a speedboat.

1 Read the next part of Alfie Small's adventure.

A Dark Cave

So I climbed aboard and paddled away. The stream got bigger and the water flowed faster, and soon I was racing along as fast as a speedboat.

I saw a huge **boulder** blocking the river. It was shaped like a dragon's head and my boat raced straight towards it. Help! I thought I was going to crash.

Then, with an awful grinding noise, the rock began to move. A dark cave opened up like a yawning mouth, and I was swept inside.

Whoosh! I whizzed along a gloomy tunnel, holding on tight as my boat zigzagged between rocks as sharp as dragon fangs.

Glossary

boulder: a large rock

The water roared and my boat spun round and round. Soon I couldn't tell which way was home.

Suddenly, I shot out of the tunnel and found myself floating on a **choppy sea**. In the distance was a small island, with a **plume** of smoke billowing up from behind some trees. I steered my boat towards it.

Nick Ward

Glossary

choppy sea: a sea with small waves

plume: a long cloud

Reading tip

Notice the exclamation marks in the passage. Think about the added expression you need to use when reading sentences that finish with exclamation marks.

Answer the questions in your notebook.

a   Did Alfie see a dragon in the water? Explain your answer.

b   Write the words Alfie uses to describe how the cave opened up.

c   What were the rocks inside the tunnel like?

d   Describe how you think Alfie felt after coming out of the tunnel.

e   Why do you think Alfie decided to head towards the island?

2   Look at the words and phrases in the passage and then read the Language focus box.

Language focus

Figurative language uses words and phrases to describe things. It helps you to imagine what they look like.

When a writer describes something by saying it is like or as something else, this is a type of figurative language called a **simile**.

Example: A dark cave opened up _like_ a yawning mouth ... between rocks _as_ sharp _as_ dragon fangs.

a Which three phrases in the box are similes?
Copy them into your notebook.

> she is a very good writer
>
> it sparkled like a diamond
>
> as exciting as watching paint dry
>
> he ran really fast
>
> as strong as an ox

b Choose one of the similes and use it in a sentence.

 3 Adding similes to a story can make that story sound very different. Listen carefully to the story about Tuhil and Meena. Talk about the scene the children come across in the woods.

 Next listen to a second version of the story. The scene is the same but the picture in your mind is different. Why?

4 What do you think happens to Alfie? Are there any clues in the text that help you guess what happens next? In your notebook, draw what you think will happen to Alfie. Label your drawing with:

- three words or phrases that tell you where Alfie was

- three words or phrases that tell you what Alfie saw

- three words or phrases that tell you what Alfie did.

> 7.4 Character portraits

We are going to...

- write about a story character.

Getting started

1 Write a description of yourself.

- Don't let anyone see what you write.
- Don't write your name!
- Put your description in the box or bowl.

2 In a group, take turns to read out the descriptions.

- Can you guess who each description is describing?

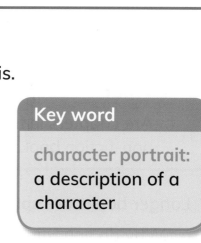

1 Would you like to be friends with Alfie Small?

Talk with a partner about the sort of person he is.

a What does he look like?

b What does he do?

c What does he think or say?

d What does he feel?

2 Write a **character portrait** of Alfie Small.

In your character portrait, use:

a interesting noun phrases to describe what Alfie looks like

b interesting verbs to describe what he thinks, does, says and writes

c different types of sentences.

> **Key word**
>
> character portrait: a description of a character

Language focus

Remember, simple sentences have one main verb: *Alfie Small* **was** an *explorer*.

Multi-clause sentences are two simple sentences joined together with a connective: *Alfie Small* **got** into his boat **and** he **paddled away**.

> ## 7.5 Looking at chapters

We are going to...

- **explore how chapters are used in books.**

Getting started

1 With a partner, look at a book that has different chapters.

2 Discuss these questions:

    a What is a chapter?

    b Are chapters in fiction books the same as chapters in non-fiction books?

1 Longer books are split into sections called chapters.

    a Why do you think writers use chapters?

    b Read these chapter headings from the book *Pirates and Dragons* by Nick Ward. Work with a partner, using the chapter headings to tell each other a story.

Chapter 1 All aboard	5
Chapter 2 A monster from the deep!	10
Chapter 3 Sizzling sausages!	15
Chapter 4 Captured!	20
Chapter 5 The hungry shark!	28
Chapter 6 Captain Alfie	38

Reading the chapter headings is a good way to see whether you might like a book. You can often guess the kind of book it is from the chapter headings.

2   The way a paragraph or chapter starts can help to make it interesting for a reader.

Language focus

Sentence openings can tell you:

* when something happens   **Example:** Later that day
* where something happens   **Example:** In the distance
* how something happens   **Example:** Slowly and carefully

a   Choose a word or phrase from the boxes to begin each new sentence.

At the end | Behind his shed | Joyfully | When he was ready

All at once | Early one morning | To his surprise | Carefully

* ... Alfie left his house and walked down his garden path.
* ... he found a stream.
* ... there was a boat.
* ... he climbed into the boat.
* ... he started to paddle.

b   Copy the finished sentences into your notebook.

> 7.6 Looking at verbs

We are going to...

- recognise past tense irregular verbs.

Getting started

1 With a partner, discuss the difference between a past tense verb and a present tense verb.

2 Try to say three past tense verbs and three present tense verbs each.

1 Read this passage from another story.

   a Who do you think wrote this story?

   b Is it like another story you have read in this unit?

The Stripy Balloon

Today, I pushed through the weeds ... and found a big, stripy balloon with a wicker basket hanging underneath.

'Come on, Jed!' I cried, jumping into the basket. I untied a rope, and the balloon rose high into the sky.

Thick, shifting clouds loomed before us. They formed into the shape of a monstrous ogre's face. Its grinning mouth opened wide and we were swept inside. Jed began to whine.

'Oh, help! Watch out, boy,' I cried, as our balloon was buffeted about, and we were thrown around the basket like clothes in a washing machine. Soon I couldn't tell which way was home.

Suddenly, we went spinning out of the cloud. Below us, everything had changed and now we were floating above a strange, rocky landscape.

Nick Ward

2 Answer these questions in your notebook.

   a What was behind the weeds?

   b Who do you think Jed is?

   c What did the cloud look like?

   d What did Jed do when the balloon went into the ogre's mouth?

   e Did you guess that the story is another story about Alfie Small? What clues did the passage give you?

   f Which creatures do you think Alfie will meet in this adventure?

   g Who do you think felt more frightened: Alfie or Jed?

   h How do you think Alfie and Jed get home?

3 Copy these verbs into your notebook.
Match the present tense verbs with their irregular past tense.

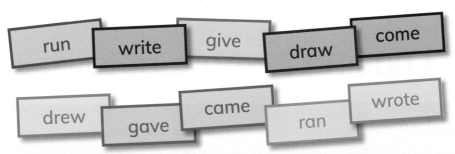

Language focus

To make the **past tense** of most verbs you add *–ed* or *–d*.

Example: look<u>ed</u>   argu<u>ed</u>

But some verb forms don't follow this rule.
They are known as irregular verbs.

Example: sing ➡ sang   go ➡ went

4 Look back at the passage in Activity 1.
List five irregular verbs you can find.

5 Plan your own Alfie Small adventure.

   a Start by writing the chapter headings.

   b Tell a partner the story you plan to write.

   c Start to write your story.

Writing tip

Remember to use:

- interesting sentence openings to show *when*, *where* and *how* events happen

- noun phrases with some good adjectives

- some multi-clause sentences with different connectives (*for example, like, because, although, when*).

〉 7.7 Looking in more detail

We are going to...

- **discuss similarities and differences in adventure stories.**

Getting started

1 Can you remember what happened in Story beginning 3 in Session 7.2 Activity 1?

2 Re-read that story beginning. Discuss with a partner what happened.

1 Story beginning 3 was taken from the book *Dragon Boy*. This is another passage from that book. Read the passage and answer the questions in your notebook.

Here, Granda is telling Lily about his father's experience in the Dragon Hills.

Fire Snatcher

'You see, Lily, the villagers needed fire to warm their homes, and cook their food, and make life good. So they chose the biggest, bravest man in the village. They gave him a fine spear and they called him Fire Snatcher. My da, your great-granda, Lily, was Fire Snatcher and hero of the village.'

'But how did he snatch the fire?' asked Lily.

'Well, Lily, dragons are strange creatures,' said Granda. 'They lay their eggs, then sleep for a full ninety years until the eggs are ready to hatch. When that happens, the dragon mothers wake up to care for their babies. The dragons were in their sleep-years when my da was Fire Snatcher. All he had to do was creep, tiptoe-quiet into the hills, then jump, suddenly, on a sleeping dragon and poke it with his spear. The poor beast would start from its sleep and blaze with fright, just as you or I would if anybody jabbed at us with a needle while we were sleeping. But it worked. It made the dragon roar fire. As it roared, the Fire Snatcher thrust his torch of dry wood into the flare of the dragon's fiery breath to light it.'

Pippa Goodhart

a List two reasons the villagers needed fire.

b How did the villagers choose the Fire Snatcher?

c Why did the Fire Snatcher need a spear?

d Why was it important the Fire Snatcher carried a torch of dry wood?

e Why do you think the Fire Snatcher needed to be brave?

f How do you think the Fire Snatchers felt about their job?

g Do you think the villagers should see the Fire Snatcher as a hero?

2 How is this adventure story the same as the stories about Alfie Small?
   How is it different? Copy and complete the table.

Similarities	Differences

3 Role play a Fire Snatcher! Imagine you have to go
   out at night to get fire from sleeping dragons.

   a How do you feel?

   b What do you see, hear and smell?

   c What do you do? How do you move?

4 With a partner, discuss these questions and
   decide on your answers.

   a Do you think this text is from a chapter near
      the beginning or near the end of the story?

   b Do you think the end of this text would be a
      good place to start a new chapter?

Listening tip

Listen to each other's
answers. Do you agree with
each other? Think about
why others might have a
different opinion. Remember
that having a different
opinion does not make an
answer wrong!

There are stories
about dragons from all around
the world. In stories from China
and India, the dragons are usually
long, snake-like creatures, with four
legs. But in stories from Europe
and America, the dragons are
shorter and have wings as
well as legs.

› 7.8 Setting and dialogue

We are going to...

- **describe a setting and use punctuation correctly.**

Getting started

1 With a partner,

    a discuss what a noun is. What are the different types of noun you know?

    b discuss what an adjective is.

2 Now, look at the setting where you are sitting.

    a Write a list of nouns that you might use to write about where you are sitting.

    b Write a list of adjectives that you might use to describe those nouns.

1 Re-read the passage from *Dragon Boy* in Session 7.7 Activity 1.

    a What did the Fire Snatcher see, hear and feel when he was in the Dragon Hills?

    b Write a paragraph describing the setting for a story about dragons.

2 Look again at the passage from *Dragon Boy* in Session 7.7 Activity 1. Read the Language focus box.

Writing tip

Remember, it is important to use interesting nouns and adjectives when describing a setting.

Language focus

Punctuate **speech** correctly.

- Use a new line for each speaker.
- Put opening speech marks (') at the beginning of the words that were said.
- Put closing speech marks (') at the end of the words that were said.
- If needed, put question marks (?) and exclamation marks (!) before the closing speech marks.
- Don't forget capital letters and full stops.

Discuss these questions.

a   How many people speak?

b   How do you know when they start and finish speaking?

c   How many times can you see the word *said*?

d   Which other word is used instead of *said*?

e   Suggest a different word that could have been used instead.

3   Copy this passage into your notebook using the correct punctuation.
Some punctuation marks are missing, others are wrong.
Write a word you could use instead of *said* in each of the gaps.

'Who was Dragon Boy? _____ Lily

Well, Lily,' _____ Granda, there
was a big fire and the villagers ran away

A mother dragon went to see if her eggs
had hatched. what do you think she saw

I don't know, _____ Lily

she found one ordinary baby dragon and another baby
he was pink and soft instead of green and scaly

I bet he was Dragon Boy, _____ Lily

What clues in the passage helped you to know when to use the correct punctuation marks?

How important is punctuation in understanding a passage?

〉 7.9 More about paragraphs

We are going to...

- **discuss the use of paragraphs and sentence openings.**

Getting started

1 Look at paragraphs in different books.

2 With a partner, discuss:

    a Why are paragraphs used in our writing?

    b How do we know when a new paragraph starts?

1 Read more of the story *Dragon Boy*.

Fire!

One day, when Dragon Boy had been huffing and puffing nothing but whistles, some young dragons began laughing at him. Dragon Boy went off sadly on his own.

As the sun began to set, Dragon Boy turned for home. But he was still so cross that he kicked angrily at the flint stones under his feet. As one struck another, Dragon Boy saw a flash of yellow.

> Here, Dragon Boy is growing up as a dragon, but he can't make fire. He just whistles.

"Fire!" shouted Dragon Boy. "I've made fire without having to breathe it!"

Quickly he began collecting dry grass and sticks and bigger logs. Then, crouching down with his back to the wind, he struck two sharp flints, one against the other. CLACK! At first the stones just smelled a little smoky.

CLACK! CLACK! CLACK! He struck them again and again, until at last a spark flashed and took to the grass. As the grass smouldered and smoked, Dragon Boy blew on it gently. He sang a fiery dragon song, and suddenly the smouldering flowered into flames.

Pippa Goodhart

2 Answer these questions in your notebook.

a Why did Dragon Boy go off by himself?

b How did he feel when he went off by himself?

c How did he first make fire?

d As Dragon Boy made the fire:

- what did he see?
- what did he smell?
- what did he hear?
- what did he feel?

e Dragon Boy did something unusual to make the fire grow. What was it?

f Which paragraph do you think is the most exciting? Why?

Reading tip

Remember, you may be able to answer some questions by scanning the passage, but you will need to read the passage in more detail to answer other questions.

3 With a partner, re-read the text and look at the Language focus box.

Language focus

Writers usually begin a **new paragraph** when they introduce a different action, a different time or a different place.

Interesting sentence openings at the beginning of each paragraph lead the reader through the story.

a Decide why the writer started new paragraphs when she did.

b Look at the sentence openings at the beginning of each paragraph. Decide if they tell the reader when, where or how an event is happening.

〉 7.10 Looking at stories

We are going to...

- write a book review, investigate prefixes and look closely at sentence openers.

Getting started

1   Would you like to read an Alfie Small book or the *Dragon Boy* book?

2   Explain why to a partner.

1   Write a review of a fiction book you have enjoyed reading. In your review, say:

   a   what you thought about the book when you read it

   b   who were the main characters and what happened to them

      (Don't say too much about what happens, or it could spoil the story for someone else.)

   c   why the reader might want to read the book.

2   What do you think the word *review* means?

How am I doing?

Read through your book review. Have you given the reader a clear impression of the book? If you hadn't read the book before, would your review have made you consider reading it?

Language focus

A **prefix** is a group of letters added before a word.

The prefix changes the meaning of the word and makes a new word.

Example: *re–* + *view* = <u>re</u>view

Each prefix adds a particular meaning to a root word.

a Copy the words into your notebook. <u>Underline</u> the prefix in each one.

return   inactive   uncover   redo   incorrect

unkind   recycle   inaccurate   unhappy

b Write a definition for each of these words.
You can use a dictionary to help you.

return   redo   unhappy   unkind   incorrect   inaccurate

c What is the meaning of:

- the prefix *re*–?
- the prefix *un*–?
- the prefix *in*–?

3 Look at this storyboard for a dragon adventure story.
Write the sentence opening for each of these paragraphs in the story.

› 7.11 Writing a story

We are going to...

- **plan and write an adventure story.**

Getting started

1 What makes a good adventure story?

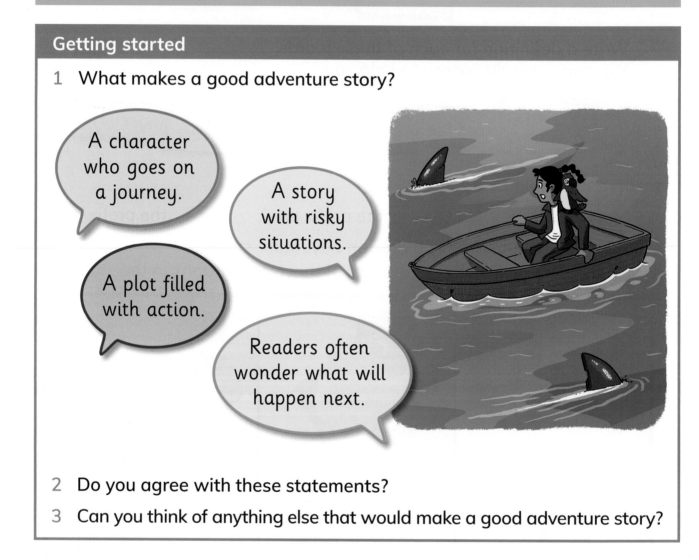

A character who goes on a journey.

A story with risky situations.

A plot filled with action.

Readers often wonder what will happen next.

2 Do you agree with these statements?

3 Can you think of anything else that would make a good adventure story?

1 Make your own adventure storyboard like the one in Session 7.10 Activity 3.

   a Use six boxes. In Box 1 write the title and in Boxes 2–6 draw pictures to show the main events.

   b Write a different sentence opening for each picture.

2   When you have finished your storyboard tell your story to a partner.
    Discuss how you could improve your story.

> **Speaking tip**
>
> Plan what you are going to say before you start speaking.
> Introduce the characters in your story first and then explain
> the adventure your character or characters are going to go
> on, a step at a time.

3   When you are happy with your storyboard, write your story.
    Remember to:

a   follow your storyboard, making sure you link the
    events so the story sequence makes sense

b   start a new chapter at the beginning of a new event

c   use paragraphs

d   use figurative language to help your reader
    imagine what things will look like

> **Writing tip**
>
> Remember, try not
> to use *said* to show
> who is talking. Use
> more interesting
> dialogue verbs.

e   use sentence openings to show the order
    of the events and how they are linked

f   say what your character sees, hears and does

g   include some dialogue and powerful words.

> 7.12 Improving your story

We are going to...

- proofread and improve our adventure story.

Getting started

Re-read the story you wrote in Session 7.11. Are you pleased with it?

1 Proofread your story.

   Read your story aloud to yourself or to a partner. Check your spelling and punctuation and make sure you haven't missed out any little words.

2 Now think about how you can improve your story.

   a Find three nouns that you could improve by choosing a better word or by adding an adjective to make a more interesting noun phrase.

   b Look at the verbs and think about the tense you used. Have you used the past tense to talk about events in the past?

   c Do the verbs match the nouns or pronouns?

3 Look at the list of points to remember in Session 7.11 Activity 3. Change at least three more things in your writing to make sure you have done everything as well as you can.

How are we doing?

Share your finished story with someone else. Ask them to comment on the things they like and ask them to suggest something you might change.

Look what I can do:

- ☐ I can discuss the different ways stories begin and predict story endings.
- ☐ I can look in more detail at the language used in a story, including noun phrases and figurative language.
- ☐ I can write about a story character.
- ☐ I can discuss the role of chapters and write paragraphs and sentence openings.
- ☐ I can explore dialogue, including the punctuation used.
- ☐ I can plan, write, proofread and improve an adventure story.

Check your progress

1 List the things that make a good adventure story.

2 Write an example of each of these parts of speech:

  a a noun

  b an adjective

  c a verb

  d a pronoun

  e a connective

3 Write a noun phrase using each of these words.

  a mountain

  b rock pool

  c boat

Continued

4   Copy and complete this sentence using figurative language (a simile).

The dragon's mouth ...

5   Copy the irregular past tense verbs in each of these sentences.

   a   The dragon had shiny, sharp scales.

   b   The dragon was green with yellow markings.

   c   The dragon smiled as he made fire spout from his mouth.

Projects

Group project: Choose an adventure story you all know. Keep the same characters as the story but role play them into a different adventure. What happens? What risky situations do they get into? Perform your role play to other groups in the class.

Pair project: Plan a storyboard for an adventure where you and your partner are the main characters in the story. What exciting things do you do? Who do you meet? What dangerous situation do you overcome? Are you still friends at the end of your adventure?

Solo project: Write a character portrait about someone you might use as the main character in an adventure story. Remember to include:

- what he or she looks like
- what he or she does
- how he or she might feel
- what he or she might think or say.

8 › Wonderful world

› 8.1 Holidays

We are going to...

- write, read and answer questions about written information.

Getting started

1 Answer these questions with a partner.

  a Where have you been on holiday?

  b What do you like doing on holiday?

  c Have you ever visited a different country?

2 Describe the holidays in these photos.

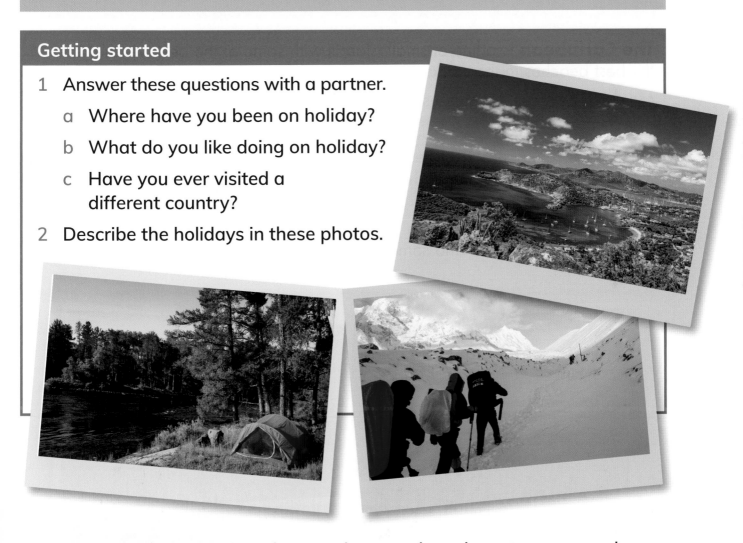

1 Write a short description about a place you have been to or somewhere you would like to go to on holiday. Describe the place as well as something that happened while you were there.

2 Read about the countries in the holiday fact file and then
   answer the questions in your notebook.

Holiday fact file

Canada is a great place for winter sports, but people also come here for the clean air and stunning scenery.

The city of Vancouver is surrounded on three sides by water and on the fourth by mountains. It also has beautiful buildings.

The Caribbean is a line of small islands with some of the best weather and the best beaches in the world.

Many cruise ships bring thousands of people to visit the islands.

Brazil has some great beaches and the city of Rio de Janeiro is famous for its carnival in the spring, when everyone dresses up and dances through the streets.

Brazil is famous for the Amazon rainforest where visitors can see enormous trees, the Amazon River and some of the rarest and most beautiful creatures on the planet.

South Africa attracts many holidaymakers, who come for its beautiful beaches and open areas of countryside, and for the safaris that allow visitors to see African animals in the wild.

With the flat-topped Table Mountain in the background, the city of Cape Town is famous for its harbour.

Australia is famous for its beaches. Many people in Australia enjoy surfing.

Australia also has the Great Barrier Reef, the world's largest coral reef. People come from all over the world to scuba dive or snorkel and to admire the fish.

China is an exciting place to visit. People come for its culture and history as well as its huge, modern cities.

The Great Wall of China is over 2000 years old and stretches over 8850 km (5500 miles). Many visitors come to walk on the wall and admire the views from it.

The United Kingdom is a little country with a lot of history. People visit to see the beautiful scenery in Scotland and Northern Ireland, ancient castles in Wales, and cities and many historical monuments in England.

India is a land of contrasts with plenty to see. In the north are the mountains of the Himalayas and in the south are beautiful beaches. In between, people can visit modern cities and ancient temples, and see farmers farming the land as they have done for centuries.

a Which place is a line of small islands?

b Which of these countries do people visit for the beaches?

c What is Brazil most famous for?

d Which countries would you visit to enjoy the scenery?

e Which countries would you visit to see interesting creatures?

f Which countries might you visit to see places from the past?

3 Write a few sentences stating which of the places in the fact file you would like to go to on holiday. Explain why.

〉 8.2 In the library

We are going to...

- look at how books in libraries are organised and organise some books alphabetically.

Getting started

1 Write these countries in alphabetical order.

Tunisia   Sri Lanka   Thailand

Spain   Mexico   Singapore

2 Share your answers with a partner. Are your answers the same?

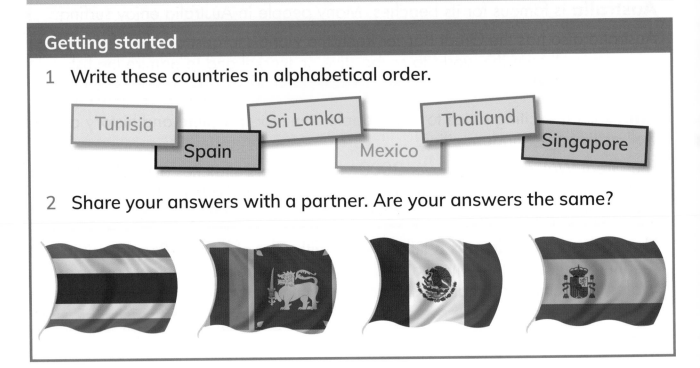

1 Look at these shelves of books in a library.

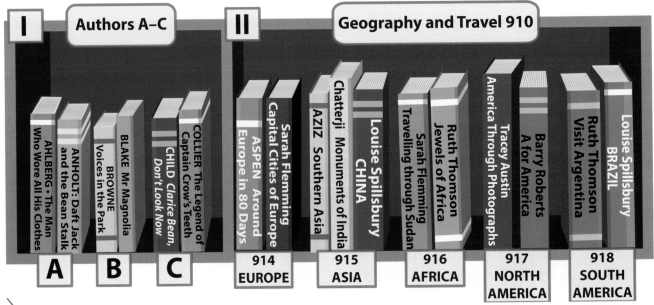

Answer the questions in your notebook.

a   Which shelf of books are fiction books and which are non-fiction books?

b   How do you know?

c   How are the books organised?

d   Where would you find a book about South Africa?

e   Where would you put a story book by Jake Broker?

f   Where would you look to find a book about where you live?

2   Read the poster about how books are organised in a school library.

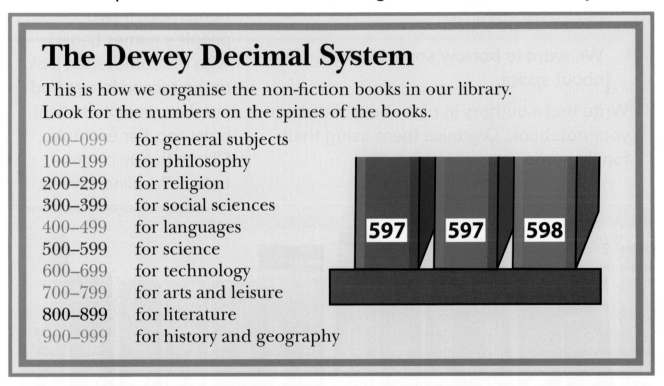

The Dewey Decimal System

This is how we organise the non-fiction books in our library.
Look for the numbers on the spines of the books.

000–099   for general subjects
100–199   for philosophy
200–299   for religion
300–399   for social sciences
400–499   for languages
500–599   for science
600–699   for technology
700–799   for arts and leisure
800–899   for literature
900–999   for history and geography

597   597   598

Reading tip

Did you know that the Dewey Decimal System is a way of classifying or organising books using numbers? It helps you find a book more easily. For example, you will find science books in the 500s section. The science section is divided again, using numbers, into various subjects, for example, books on plants (580–589) or animals (590–599). Then these are subdivided into topics – such as fish (597) or birds (598).

Look at the different types of information needed by learners. What numbers would these learners need to look for to find books with this information? Write the numbers in your notebook.

a I need help with my French homework. 400–499

b We want to find out about Africa.

c I'd like to know about the lifecycle of a frog.

d We are doing a project on religions.

e I am interested in the paintings of Leonardo da Vinci.

f We want to borrow some books about space.

3 Write these authors in alphabetical order in your notebook. Organise them using their family name.

Pippa Goodhart · Colin McNaughton · A.A. Milne · Roald Dahl · Laurence Anholt · Jill Murphy · Francesca Simon · Anne Fine · Michael Morpurgo · Martin Waddell · Alfie Smith · Jacqueline Wilson · Rose Impey · Jon Scieszka

› 8.3 Inside a non-fiction book

We are going to...

- **discuss in detail what is found in a non-fiction book.**

Getting started

1 Write a list of the differences between a non-fiction and a fiction book.

2 Compare your list with a partner's.

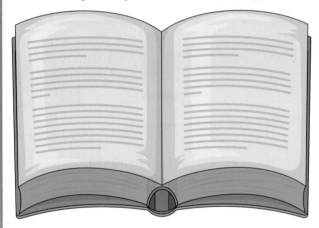 

1 Look at the texts on the next page. They are from a book about Caribbean islands.

   a Where in the book would you find these pages?

   b How are they organised?

Reading tip

The contents page tells you the main headings and topics in the book.

The index tells you where to find out about particular subjects, names or ideas.

Contents

Index

2 Answer these questions in your notebook.

   a Which page would you look at to find information about volcanoes?

   b Which topic is on pages 10–11?

   c Which subjects, names or ideas can you find out more about on pages 10–11?

   d Which sports do they play in the Caribbean?

   e What is page 17 about?

   f Puerto Rico is discussed under two topics. What are they?

3 Non-fiction books give information in lots of different ways. Look at the Language focus box. Browse some non-fiction books and find the different features. Talk about what you find with a partner.

Language focus

In **non-fiction** texts:

- the **heading** tells you what the topic is

- the **text** gives information about the topic

- if the text is quite long, **subheadings** tell you where the different bits of the topic are talked about

- the **photographs**, **illustrations** and **diagrams** give you information using pictures not words

- a **caption** is a short explanation of what is in a picture

- a **label** names part of a diagram

- some of the information might be given in a list, with or without **bullet points**

- there might be a **glossary** to tell you what some of the difficult words mean.

Reading tip

Browsing means having a quick look through a text, without spending time reading all the words carefully. Here are some ways to browse a book.

- Look at the covers. What can you learn from: the title? The pictures? The blurb?
- Open the book and quickly read the contents page.
- Flick through the book, looking at the pictures.

Browsing lets you get an idea of what the book is about so that you can decide whether you want to read it.

> 8.4 Skimming and scanning

We are going to...

- discuss different ways of reading a text.

Getting started

1 Pick up any non-fiction book. Look at it for a couple of minutes.

2 With a partner discuss what you like or don't like about the book.

3 How did you decide what you did or didn't like?

1 Read this text aloud.

Seasons in the Caribbean

There are two seasons in the Caribbean: a wet season and a dry season. Each season lasts for about six months.

The wet season is the season of rain. The wet season starts in about June and goes on until November. The rain is usually heavier inland, nearer the mountains.

During the wet season there are more **tropical** storms and hurricanes. Hurricanes are very, very strong winds, with heavy rain. There are usually about eight hurricanes each year.

There is less rain during the dry season which lasts from December to May. Tourists come to the islands then to enjoy the beautiful Caribbean beaches in the hot sun.

Glossary

tropical: where the weather is warm/hot and wet

a How did you read the text?

b Did you skim, scan or read slowly and carefully?

Reading tip

There are different ways of reading.

- **Skim** a text to get the main idea.
- **Scan** to find a particular word or piece of information.
- **Read slowly and carefully** to understand the text fully.

2 Answer these questions in your notebook.

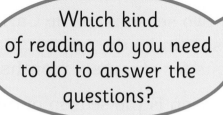

a How many times can you find these words in the text in Activity 1?

- season (or seasons)
- *hurricane (or hurricanes)*
- Caribbean?

Which kind of reading do you need to do to answer the questions?

b When is the dry season?

c Where is rain heaviest on the islands?

d When do hurricanes occur? How many of them are there each year?

e How would you know if you were in a hurricane?

f If you were going to the Caribbean, which month of the year would you like to visit? Why?

3 Look at a non-fiction book with a partner.
Write questions for each other about the information in the book.
Do you have to use different kinds of reading to find the answers?

4 Look at these sentences from a non-fiction book. Choose the correct verbs and write the complete sentences in your notebook.

a Whales (*swim / swims*) in the waters of the South Pacific Ocean near Chile.

b They (*pass / passes*) Chile as they (*look / looks*) for food.

c A boat (*take / takes*) people out to sea.
They (*want / wants*) to see the whales.

d Other animals (*live / lives*) in Chile too.

e The Atacama desert (*is / are*) in Chile.
It (*is / are*) the driest place on Earth.

f At night, reptiles (*burrow / burrows*) underground in the desert. In the day, they (*lie / lies*) on rocks and (*get / gets*) warm.

› 8.5 Using paragraphs

We are going to...

- **discuss different types of sentences and write some paragraphs.**

Getting started

1 Re-read the text about seasons in the Caribbean in Session 8.4 Activity 1.

   a Why is the text divided into paragraphs?

   b What is the main idea in each paragraph?

2 Look at some more non-fiction books.
   Find the main idea in some of the paragraphs.

---

1 Choose a topic you know about.

   a Think of **two** different ideas you would like to write about that topic.

   b Write a paragraph about each of the ideas.

2 Copy these sentence beginnings into your notebook. Complete them as multi-clause sentences.

   a I would like to visit the Caribbean ...

   b We can visit the white beaches ...

   c It is beautiful in the dry season ...

A new paragraph usually means there is a new subject or idea.

Language focus

Remember, a **multi-clause sentence** can be made up of two simple sentences joined with a **connective**.

A connective is used to join sentences.
Connectives can reflect time, place or cause.

Example:

time connectives =	*first*	*next*	*last*	*then*
place connectives =	*up*	*over*	*behind*	
cause connectives =	*so*	*if*	*because*	

3 Copy these sentence beginnings into your notebook. Add conditional clauses to complete them as conditional sentences.

   a I would like to visit the Caribbean ...

   b We can visit the white beaches ...

   c It is beautiful in the dry season ...

Language focus

We can make paragraphs more exciting by using different types of sentences.

Conditional sentences are made up of a main clause and a *conditional* clause. Conditional clauses usually begin with *if* or *unless* and can come before or after the main clause.

Example:

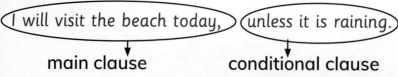

I will visit the beach today,   *unless it is raining.*

    main clause   conditional clause

〉 8.6 Language features of information texts

We are going to...

- look in detail at language features and investigate the difference between fact and opinion in information texts.

Getting started

With a partner, discuss which of these sentences you think are facts and which are opinions.

I am 7 years old.

One day I want to visit Australia.

I am going to be a fast runner.

I love riding my bike.

1 Read the paragraph about Australia.

a Answer the questions in your notebook.

Australia fact file

The centre of Australia is a huge desert called the Outback. It is very dry and flat with red earth. In the middle of the Outback there is a town called Alice Springs. Many tourists visit Alice Springs because they want to see the mountain-sized rock known as Uluru, probably the most dramatic natural feature in the country. Uluru is the traditional Aboriginal name for it, but it was once known as Ayers Rock, an English name given to it in the 19th century. People have lived near Uluru for over 10 000 years. It is a spiritual place for many. It is one piece of sandstone rock that is approximately 3.6 km long and 1.9 km wide.

52

The climb to the top is over 1.6 km, up a steep slope. When people were allowed to climb the rock, most found it a tough climb. However, tourists are no longer allowed to climb the rock, but they can walk around its base. A stunning time to see Uluru is at sunset.

- What is the main idea in this paragraph?
- What heading would you give the paragraph?
- Which **tense** is the writing in?
- What other name was Uluru once given?
- Why do you think people are interested in Uluru?
- List any words in the text that you don't know the meaning of.

Key word

tense: the time described by a verb, for example, present or past

b Can you work out what they might mean from the other information in the text?

c Check their meanings in a dictionary or online.

2 Read the Language focus box. Answer the questions about the information on Australia in Activity 1.

Language focus

Non-fiction writing includes *facts* and sometimes *opinions*.

A **fact** is something that is known to be true.

An **opinion** is someone's thoughts on something, but it isn't always based on facts.

a How many facts can you count?

b List two examples of facts.

c List two examples of opinions.

d Why do you think information texts have more facts than opinions?

3 Talk with a partner about the language used in the text in Activity 1.

  a What tense is the text written in?

  b List any powerful verbs.

  c List any interesting adjectives.

4 Answer these questions about the text in Activity 1 in your notebook.

> **Listening tip**
>
> Take turns to listen to each other's suggestions. Respond politely to each other.

  a Find the verbs in the text. Which verb is used most?

  b Write the adjectives in the text. Do they help give more facts?

  c Which pronouns can you find in the text? Can you find the pronouns *I, you* or *we*?

  d List the prepositions you can find in the text.

  e What punctuation can you find in the text? Are there any question marks or exclamation marks? Why do you think this is?

Remember, prepositions are words that show the relationship between a noun (or pronoun) with another word in the sentence. They often can show the 'position' of something.
on   under   behind

Think about your writing. What language do you use in your non-fiction writing? What about your fiction writing? Is the language different?

> 8.7 Non-fiction e-texts

We are going to...

- **discuss e-texts and how they are different from books.**

Getting started

1 What is an e-text?

2 Where do you find e-texts?

3 What does the e in 'e-text' stand for?

4 Make a mind-map of your ideas with a partner.

1 Read the fact file.

 e-text fact file

An e-text is an electronic text – that just means it's a text on a screen, not in a book. You will find most of the same text features in non-fiction e-texts as you do in non-fiction books. Here are some features you only find in e-texts:

> You may be able to hear the text read aloud.

> You may be able to look at videos as well as photographs.

> If you click on a highlighted word or image, you may be shown more information about it.

> You can print the screen – and you may be able to add your own notes to the text first.

> You may be able to email the text to your friends.

Reading tip

You find e-texts on the internet and you read them on computers, tablets, ebook readers or mobile phones.

Discuss these questions with a partner.

a   When did you last read an e-text to find information?

b   Look at a web page with a partner. List the features of e-texts as you look at information on the web page.

2   Look at a non-fiction e-text and a non-fiction book. Answer these questions in your notebook.

a   Are the paragraphs used in the same way?

b   Can you skim and scan the e-text to find information quickly?

c   Can you skim and scan the book to find information quickly?

d   Is the way that you find the information the same in both texts?

Using the internet safely

- Make sure an adult can see what you are doing.

- Ask an adult before you visit any new websites.

- Ask for help if you're not sure what to do.

- Never give your full name, your school, your address or your phone number on the internet.

- Tell an adult if you see or read anything that makes you feel uncomfortable.

The internet is useful and fun if you use it safely.

3 Choose a country you would like to find out more about.

a Use books or the internet to research this country.

b Write a list of words you might use when writing about this country, for example:

AUSTRALIA

an island

the outback

Uluru

beaches

desert

Sydney Opera House

> 8.8 Planning a talk

We are going to...

- **plan a talk in a group.**

Getting started

1 List different subjects you find interesting.

2 Choose one of the subjects. Or you can select one of these:

birds   Brazil   cricket   cooking

3 Think of as many questions as you can that are linked with this subject.

1 You are going to find out about a subject and give a talk about it.

   a Look at the table. Can you see how the subject 'Norway' has been split into topics?

   b Work in a group and choose a different subject for a talk.

Subject: NORWAY	
Topics and questions	**Answers**
Geography Where is it? Which other countries are nearby?	In northern Europe – Scandinavia Sweden, Denmark, Finland, Poland, Germany, UK
Cities What is the capital city? What do people go and see in the cities?	Oslo. Nearly 1 million people live there. Viking ship museum – Vikings came from Norway Sculpture park People don't usually go there for the cities
Countryside What does it look like? What do people do in the countryside?	Lots of fjords (say 'fee-ords') where the sea goes far inland The north is in the Arctic Circle with reindeer (called caribou); it's called 'the land of the midnight sun' because the sun doesn't set in summer Skiing in winter Whale watching in the Atlantic Climb glaciers (frozen rivers or masses of ice)

2 Once you have found a subject you all agree on, complete these tasks.

   a Copy a blank version of the table into your notebook
      and write in the subject your group has chosen.

   b Split the subject into topics and decide who will research each topic.
      Your topics might be different from the ones on Norway.

   c Write some questions that you want to
      answer for each topic.

3 Do your research.

   a Use books and e-texts to find the
      information you need.

   b Make notes of interesting information
      in the 'Answers' column of your table.

> **Reading tip**
>
> When you look for information, decide if you need to skim, scan or read carefully.

> 8.9 Giving your talk

We are going to...

- **give a talk on a subject we have chosen.**

Getting started

1 In pairs, practise reading a short paragraph aloud to each other.

   a Try to speak clearly and confidently.

   b Make eye contact with the person you are talking to.

2 Ask your partner for feedback on what you might improve.

1 Listen carefully to a talk on Norway.

   Read the Speaking tip.

   a Do the speakers achieve all the points made in the Speaking tip?

   b How could the talk be improved?

   c Can you think of any questions you might ask?

Speaking tip

When you give a talk:

- begin with a clear statement about what the talk will be about

- introduce each part of the talk separately, with its own heading

- give most of the talk in the present tense

- try to give information your listeners will be interested in

- talk with expression, making your voice interesting to listen to

- speak clearly and confidently, making eye contact with your listeners.

2   Before you present your talk, practise giving it with your group.

Work together to improve the talk.

3   Give your talk to the class. Try to answer any questions your listeners ask at the end.

Listen politely and with interest to the other talks. Think of some questions you could ask at the end.

Don't forget to say what the subject of your talk is first. Relax and enjoy yourself when you give your talk.

How am I doing?

Are you pleased with how your talk went? Why or why not? What can you improve next time?

› 8.10 Planning an information text

We are going to...

- **plan, research and record information for an information text.**

Getting started

Look back at the texts in this unit. What is the same about them? What is different? Look at:

- the type of information they give
- the language
- how they are organised into paragraphs
- the headings, subheadings, pictures, captions and labels.

1 Choose a country to write an information text about.

Write four key questions you want to answer in your information text.

2 How will you record your research?

You could use a table like the one in Session 8.8 Activity 1.

Draw your plan.

3 Research your subject using books and e-texts.

Make notes for each key area you are researching.

Remember how you researched the talk you gave in the previous session. What skills did you use? What resources gave you the most information?

> 8.11 Writing an information text

We are going to...

- **follow a plan and write an information text.**

Getting started

1 Ask a partner to read through the planning sheet you wrote in Session 8.10.

2 Is there anything else they think you could include?

1 Look at the planning sheet you wrote in the previous session.

   Check you have included interesting things the readers will want to know about.

2 Write your information text. Remember to:

   - follow your plan

   - write in paragraphs, starting a new paragraph for each new topic or idea

   - use headings for each section

   - give interesting information

   - use simple, multi-clause and conditional sentences with different connectives

   - keep the tense the same and make sure the nouns and pronouns match the verbs.

> Which country did you write about? Can you find it on a map?

Writing tip

Write by hand or type your information text neatly.
Add pictures, diagrams or maps that relate to what you have written to make your information more interesting to the reader.

› 8.12 Improving your text

We are going to...

- **improve the information text we have written.**

Getting started

By reading things aloud, you often notice things that are missing or could be written better.

Read your information text aloud to yourself.

What do you notice?

1 Proofread your text.

Check the following and change your writing if you need to.

a Check your spelling. List any words you are unsure of. Check these words in a dictionary.

b Check your punctuation and make sure you haven't missed out any little words.

c Look at the verbs. Have you used the present tense all the way through?
Do the verbs match the nouns or pronouns?

d Are there any sentences that you could join together?

2 Check how you have organised your information.

a Have you used useful headings and are they in the right places?

b Do you need to add new information or move information to a different paragraph?

How are we doing?

Read your information text aloud to a partner.
Ask your partner if they find the information interesting.
Is there anything else they think you could include?

3   When you have checked everything, present your text attractively for display.

Check your text again to make sure it is as good as possible.

Look what I can do!

- [ ] I can read and answer questions about written information.
- [ ] I can understand how books in libraries are organised.
- [ ] I can look at features found in non-fiction texts and investigate the difference between fact and opinion.
- [ ] I can discuss e-texts and how they are different from books.
- [ ] I can plan and give a talk on a chosen subject.
- [ ] I can plan, research, write and improve an information text.

Check your progress

1 What is the difference between paragraphs in stories and paragraphs in information texts?

2 What is the difference between the language in stories and the language in information texts?

3 What are the most important things to remember when writing information texts?

4 Copy and finish these sentences so they are multi-clause or conditional sentences.

   a In Australia the cities are near the coast ...

   b Alice Springs is one of the closest towns to Uluru ...

   c Hurricanes happen in the Caribbean ...

5 Choose the correct verbs to go with the nouns or pronouns. Then write the sentences in your notebook.

   a Whales (*swim / swims*) in the South Atlantic.

   b They (*are / is*) feeding.

   c People (*go / goes*) out in boats to watch them.

Continued

    d They sometimes (*have / has*) to travel a long way.

    e Whales (*travels / travel*) even further.

6 Write two sentences; one that is a fact and one that is opinion.

Projects

Group project: Organise the books in your school or class to make a library. If your school already has a library, check how well it is organised.

Remember to have separate shelves for fiction and non-fiction books.

Look up more information on the Dewey Decimal System to make sure you are putting the books in the correct categories.

Pair project: Choose a subject both you and your partner find interesting but don't know much about. For 15 minutes, research as much information as you can on the subject.

See who can find the most interesting facts. Choose the best information to write an information text on the subject.

Solo project: Write a fact file about where you live. First write notes and questions to help you decide what you might include in the fact file. Think about what would encourage people to come and see the area.

Make your fact file look as interesting as possible.

9 > Laughing allowed

> 9.1 Riddles

We are going to...

- explore how the use of words can make things funny.

Getting started

1 What makes you laugh?

| Things you see? | Things you hear? |

With a partner, talk about what makes something funny.

2 Tell your partner a **riddle** or a **joke**.
Does it make your partner smile or laugh?

Which side of a tiger has more stripes?

I don't know. Which side of a tiger has more stripes?

The outside!

Key words

riddle: a question that describes something in a confusing way and has a clever or funny answer

joke: something that is said or read that makes someone smile or laugh

1 With a partner, read these jokes and riddles.

Discuss which of them you think is the funniest. Why?

Where do wise fish keep their money?

In a river bank.

What can you never make right, no matter how hard you try?

What flies all day but never gets anywhere?

A flag.

Your left foot.

Language focus

A **pun** is a play on words. Puns can be found in riddles, jokes and poems and they can make them funny.

Puns use a word that has several meanings or that sounds like another word (*homophone*). They work because you expect the word to mean one thing but then it turns out to mean something else.

Continued

Example:

Why do bees have sticky hair?
They use honeycombs!

A <u>honeycomb</u> is something you find in a beehive, but a <u>comb</u> is something you comb your hair with.

Other puns work because you change a word, or part of a word, to sound like another.

Example:

What do you call a dinosaur that's a noisy sleeper?
A bronto-snorus!

Instead of <u>brontosaurus</u>, you have the made-up word <u>bronto-snorous</u> – the <u>snore</u> bit makes you think of someone who snores.

2 Re-read the jokes and riddles in Activity 1.

Write a sentence explaining the pun in each one.

3 Do you know other jokes or riddles with puns?

Say one to a partner. Can they explain the pun used?

Key word

punch line:
the last part
of the joke
or riddle that
makes it funny

Speaking tip

When you say jokes or riddles aloud, you need to leave a short pause before the **punch line**. This gives the listener time to try and work out the answer.

4 Read the Language focus box about homonyms.
Then answer the questions.

Language focus

A **homonym** is a type of homophone.

A homonym is spelled the same as another word but has a different meaning, for example:

ring *a band you wear on your finger*

something round in shape

Some puns work because of homonyms.

a   Copy these homonyms into your notebook. Beside each homonym write two sentences that show two different meanings of the word.

bark   light   watch   bat   sink

b   List any homonyms in the riddles and jokes in Activity 1.

> 9.2 Wordplay in poetry

We are going to...

- **look in detail at a poem and the words it uses.**

Getting started

1   List as many words as you can that rhyme with these words:

cat   gold   clean

2   Compare your list with a partner.

Who has found the most words?

1   Read *Wordspinning*. Then answer the questions in your notebook.

Wordspinning

Spin pins into nips.
Snap pans into naps.
Mix spit into tips.
Turn parts into traps.

Switch post into stop.
Whisk dear into dare.
Carve hops into shop.
Rip rate into tear.

Twist tame into mate.
Make mean into name.
Juggle taste into state
In the wordspinning game.

John Foster

pins   tear
rate   mean
nips   name
parts   tame
tips   dare
post   game

a   Find two words the poet uses with the same letters as *spin*.

b   List three pairs of words that rhyme.

c   Apart from the last line, what type of word does each line of
    the poem start with?

d   Which two rhyming words don't use the same spelling pattern?

e   List any words in the poem that are homophones or homonyms.

2   Most lines in the poem start with a verb in the present tense.
    Write each verb in its past tense form.

Remember,
the **past tense** form of
regular verbs ends in **–ed**.
danc**ed**
Other verbs, called **irregular verbs**,
don't follow this rule and have different
past tense forms.
run   ran

3 Read the tongue twisters.
   Read each one three times, as fast as you can.

Whether the Weather

Whether the weather be fine

Or whether the weather be not

Whether the weather be cold

Or whether the weather be hot –

We'll weather the weather

Whatever the weather

Whether we like it or not!

Anonymous

She sells seashells on the seashore.

Peter Piper picked a peck of pickled peppers.

Red lorry, yellow lorry. Red lolly, yellow lolly.

a Why do you think they are called tongue twisters?

b Write a definition of a tongue twister in your notebook.

> **Reading tip**
>
> **Alliteration** is when you use the same sound at the beginning of several words that are close together. It can make things difficult to read, but if you start reading slowly and then speed up it becomes easier.

4   Reread the poems *Wordspinning* (Activity 1) and *Whether the Weather* (Activity 3).

   a   Think about the different ways the poets play with words.

   b   Choose one of the poems and practise reading it aloud until you can recite it without having to look at it. Add some actions.

> **Speaking tip**
>
> Read aloud with expression.
>
> Emphasise the important words.
>
> Read the poems with rhythm.

> 9.3 Funny poems and limericks

We are going to...

- **discuss what makes different poems funny.**

Getting started

With a partner, list all the things a poem might need to make it funny.

1   Read the poems. Then answer the questions in your notebook.

Starter

Hi!

I'm cousin Art

And I like to start

A new thing every day.

But I never finish anything

At least that's what …

they …

Tony Bradman

The Monster

Some are ugly,

Some are tall,

Some are scary,

Some are small.

Some are difficult to see.

And some are in my family.

Emma Hjeltnes

a   Why is the first poem titled *Starter*?

b   Why has the poet left out the last word in the poem *Starter*?

c   What word is missing from the last line of *Starter*?

d   Write three of the adjectives that describe monsters in *The Monster*.

e   Why is the last line of *The Monster* funny?

f   Which poem do you like best? Why?

> If you met the poets who wrote these poems, what would you ask them? Can you think of three questions you would ask each poet?

2   Listen to the poem Crazy Days two or three times. Talk about why it is funny. Answer the questions with a partner.

Listening tip

Each time you listen to the poem, focus your mind on something different. Listen to what the words are saying. Listen to the rhythm. Listen to the rhyming words.

a   What is clever about the poem?

b   How many verses does the poem have?

c   How do you know a new verse is starting?

d   Each verse has four lines. Listen carefully. Which two lines of each verse rhyme?

e   With a partner, write your own verse for this poem. Remember:

- it needs to be nonsense!

- start the verse with 'Twas.

- two lines need to rhyme.

How do you think saying poems aloud might improve them? Has it improved any poem you have ever written.

3 Read the limerick *There Was an Old Man With a Beard*.
Then talk about what makes it a funny poem.

Language focus

A limerick is a funny poem with five lines.

All limericks have the same rhythm and rhyme pattern.

Lines 1, 2 and 5 rhyme, and lines 3 and 4 rhyme.

There Was an Old Man With a Beard

There was an old man with a beard

Who said, 'It is just as I feared! –

Two owls and a hen,

Four larks and a wren,

Have all built their nests in my beard!'

Edward Lear

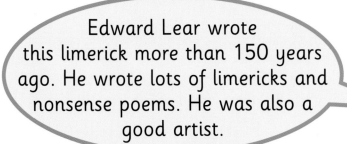

Edward Lear wrote this limerick more than 150 years ago. He wrote lots of limericks and nonsense poems. He was also a good artist.

4   Look at the limerick with gaps.

   a   With a partner, decide what other words could complete the lines of the limerick.

   b   Choose the three most important words from your poem. Explain why you chose them.

> There was _____ with a beard
>
> Who said, ' _____ I feared! –
>
> _____ and a hen,
>
> _____ and a wren,
>
> _____ in my beard!'

> ## 9.4 Calligrams and mnemonics

We are going to...

- **look at different ways to remember the spelling of words.**

Getting started

1   With a partner, discuss different ways that help you to remember how to spell words. Think of as many different ways as possible.

2   Can computers also help you to spell words correctly? How?

1   Read the poem and answer the questions in your notebook.

Kite

I'm
part of a
project on flight.
I'm supposed to attain
a great height. But
unfortunately
I got stuck
in a tree
so
it
looks
like
I'm
here
for
the
night!

June Crebbin

a   Why do you think the poet wrote her poem in this shape?

b   Why had someone made the kite?

c   What does *attain a great height* mean?

d   What happened to the kite?

e   What do you think will happen next?

The poem *Kite* is a calligram. Calligram poems are also known as shape poems.

2 Some words have the same sound but use different letters.

   a Look at the word *stuck* in the poem. Say the word aloud.

   b Find another word in the poem with the same ck sound.

   c Copy and underline the consonants that make the same sound in these words:

3 Read the language focus box. Talk about the calligram words.

Language focus

A **calligram** is a poem or word arranged on the page to make a picture or shape. The picture shows the theme of the poem or the meaning of the word.

Drawing the shape of a word can sometimes help you remember how to spell a word or its meaning.

   a How could calligrams help you to remember spellings and meanings?

   b Choose three words and write them as calligrams.

4 Read the mnemonics in the Language focus box.
Do you think they would be helpful?

Language focus

A **mnemonic** is a saying which helps you to remember the spelling of a word or a fact.

Examples:

because = **b**ig **e**lephants **c**an **a**lways **u**nderstand **s**maller **e**lephants.

points of the compass – North, East, South and West = **N**aughty **E**lephants **S**quirt **W**ater.

friend = A really good fri**end** stays right until the **end**.

said = **S**ally-**A**nne **is d**ancing.

5 Write a mnemonic to help you remember how to spell two of these words.

want   eight   was   laugh

Writing tip

It is a good idea to keep a log of words you find difficult to spell. It means you have somewhere to look back to if you need to spell those words again.

› 9.5 Reviewing a poem

We are going to...

- write a review of a poem.

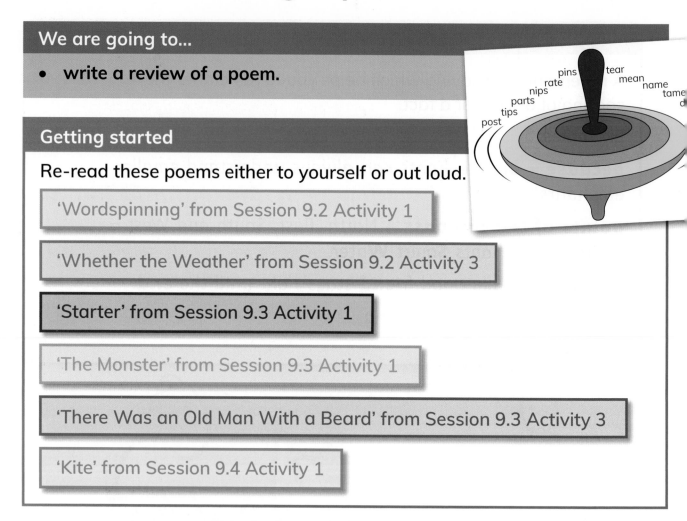

Getting started

Re-read these poems either to yourself or out loud.

'Wordspinning' from Session 9.2 Activity 1

'Whether the Weather' from Session 9.2 Activity 3

'Starter' from Session 9.3 Activity 1

'The Monster' from Session 9.3 Activity 1

'There Was an Old Man With a Beard' from Session 9.3 Activity 3

'Kite' from Session 9.4 Activity 1

1 Choose three of these poems.

Copy and complete this table in your notebook.

Name of poem	Favourite line in poem	What I like about this poem	What I don't like about this poem

2 Write a review for one of the poems.

Remember to:

- include the title of the poem
- describe the type of poem
- describe what the poem is about
- say how the poem made you feel
- say if it was a serious or funny poem
- explain why others might enjoy the poem.

3 It is a good idea to keep a list of words you find difficult to spell.

Look back at your review.

a In your notebook, list any words you think you may have spelled incorrectly.

b Check these words in a dictionary or on a computer.

c Add the words you find tricky to spell to your spelling log. Add the correct spelling of these words to the list in your notebook.

How are we doing?

Give your review to a partner. Do they agree with your review? Would they have included anything else?

> 9.6 Writing and performing a poem

We are going to...

- **write and perform a poem.**

Getting started

Describe each of these types of poems:

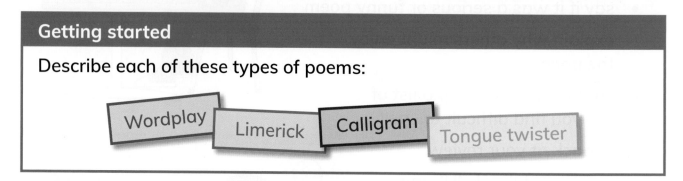

Wordplay Limerick Calligram Tongue twister

1   Choose a type of poem you have learnt about in this unit.

Write your own poem in the same style.

a   Think about what your poem will be about.
Write a list of ideas and choose the best one.

b   Write words you might use in your poem.

c   Write your poem. You may have to try different words
or lines before your poem sounds right.

Writing tip

Choosing words in poems is more difficult than choosing words in stories. When you choose words for poems, make sure they:

- make sense
- tell the reader what you want them to know
- fit the rhythm of the poem
- fit the rhyme of the poem (if there is one).

2 Read your poem to a partner.
   Can they help you to improve it?
   You should both think about:

   - the wordplay
   - the sounds of the words
   - the rhythm and rhyme
   - your choice of words – could you choose better adjectives or stronger verbs?

   Don't forget to check your spelling!

3 Practise performing your poem. Read it aloud several times, thinking about the sounds, rhythm, rhyme and meaning. Are there actions you can add while performing your poem to make it more entertaining? When you are happy with it, perform your poem.

How am I doing?

Did you enjoy the performance? What went well?
What could have been even better?
Did you include actions in your performance?
Did they make it more entertaining for the audience?

Look what I can do!

- ☐ I can explore how the use of words can make things funny.
- ☐ I can look in detail at a poem and the words it uses.
- ☐ I can discuss what makes a poem funny.
- ☐ I can look at different ways to remember the spelling of words.
- ☐ I can write a review of a poem.
- ☐ I can write and perform a poem.

Check your progress

1 Which type of poem or wordplay used:

  a rhythm?

  b rhyme?

  c puns?

  d sounds?

2 How many lines does a limerick have?

3 Write the two meanings of the word *dear*.

4 Write a calligram word.

5 Write a mnemonic for the word *separate*.

Projects

Group project: Find a funny poem and learn it off by heart. Decide as a group who will say which lines and how they will be performed. You might decide to split your group in two with more than one person reciting the words in a line. Will you use any actions?

Perform your poem.

Pair project: With a partner, create your own tongue twister. Try out different ideas and agree on the best one.

How quickly can you say your tongue twister?
How many times can you say it without making a mistake?

Solo project: Choose a poem you have written, or a poem you enjoy reading.

Copy the poem.

- Will you type or handwrite it?
- Will you place it at the top, middle or bottom of the page?
- Will you include a calligram?
- How will you illustrate it?

› Term 1 Spelling activities

1 Compound words

Compound words are words made up of two shorter words:

break + fast = breakfast   tooth + brush = toothbrush
extra + ordinary = extraordinary

a   In your notebook write as many compound words as you
can using these words:

any   every   some   no   one   body   where   thing   more

b   Write these animal words as compound word sums, for example:
bull + frog = bullfrog

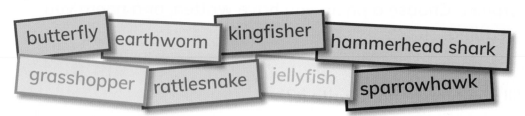

butterfly   earthworm   kingfisher   hammerhead shark
grasshopper   rattlesnake   jellyfish   sparrowhawk

2 Spelling strategies

If you don't know how to spell a word, you could:

- use a phoneme frame to divide it up into its sounds like this:

sh	ar	p

- think of a similar word you know how to spell, for example
  catch ⟶ match

- think about prefixes and suffixes you already know.

Spell these words. The words in the brackets will help.

a   b   c

(eight)   (measure)   (nature)

3 Alphabetical order

Dictionaries and other lists of words are often organised in alphabetical order. All the words beginning with A are first, followed by the words beginning with B, then C and so on. If the first letters of the word are the same, order the words according to their second letters.

a Copy and complete the alphabet in your notebook:

a b __ d e __ __ h i j __ l m __ o __ q r __ __ u v __ x __ z

b Copy and complete the alphabet in capital letters in your notebook:

__ B C __ E F G __ I J __ L __ __ O P Q __ S __ U __ W __ Y Z

c Write these animal names in alphabetical order.

penguin tortoise fox bear seal fish tiger lion

4 Spelling rules

Knowing rules about spelling can help you to make the right choices when you are writing. (But remember that English is a funny language and there are a few words that don't obey these rules.)

Rules for adding –s, –ing and –ed to verbs

Word	Verb	+ –s	+ –ing	+ –ed
For most verbs, just add the new ending.	walk	walks	walking	walked
For verbs that end in *e*, add the –s, but chop off the *e* before adding –ed or –ing.	change	changes	changing	changed

Word	Verb	+ −s	+ −ing	+ −ed
For verbs with a short vowel followed by a single consonant, add the s, but double the consonant before adding −ing or −ed.	clap	claps	clapping	clapped

Copy and complete this table in your notebook.

Verb	+ −s	+ −ing	+ −ed
push	pushes		
	smiles		
knot			
			grinned
		circling	

5 Same letters, different sounds

Some words use the same letters, but those letters make different sounds.

love   **m**ove

a   Match each word in the first box with a word in the second box that has the same letters but that makes a different sound. Watch out! You will not need to use all the words in the second box. Write the pairs of words in your notebook.

> **Speaking tip**
>
> Say the words out loud to clearly hear which words make different sounds.

glove
cough
bruise
weight
catalogue
mallet
eight

move
tongue
wallet
trough
shove
dough
height
guide

b   <u>Underline</u> the letter string in each pair of words.

⟩ Term 2 Spelling activities

1 Spelling strategies

If you don't know how to spell a word, you could:

- use a phoneme frame to divide it up into its sounds
- think of a similar word you know how to spell, for example *belief* ⟶ *brief*
- think about prefixes and suffixes you already know
- count the syllables and spell each syllable separately
- think about a spelling rule you already know.

Use some of these strategies to spell these words.

a  **b**  **c**  **d**

2 Contractions

Contractions use an apostrophe to show where a letter, or letters, have been missed out. The apostrophe takes the place of the missing letter or letters.

do n**o**t = don't   I **wi**ll = I'll

a Write contractions for these words.

he will   it is   they are

b Now write each contraction you have written into a sentence.

3 Homophones

A **homophone** is a word that sounds the same as another word but has a different meaning and spelling (for example, *dear = deer*).

a Write a homophone for each of these words.

one past board here piece

b Write two homophones for each of these words.

they're too

4 Suffixes

A suffix is a group of letters added at the end of a word. Most suffixes change the kind of word it is.

The suffixes –ful and –less can change nouns into adjectives, sometimes with opposite meanings (for example, *thoughtful* and *thoughtless*).

a Write the opposite of these adjectives by changing the suffix.

careful harmless thankful doubtless
hopeful painless colourless powerless

The suffix –ment can change a verb into a noun (for example, *agree* ⟶ *agreement*).

The suffix –ness can change an adjective into a noun (for example, *kind* ⟶ *kindness*).

b Change these verbs and adjectives into nouns by adding a suffix.

appoint attach aware bright clever develop embarrass

The suffix –ly can change adjectives into adverbs (for example, *quick* ⟶ *quickly*).

The suffix –ous can change nouns into adjectives
(for example, *poison* ⟶ *poisonous*).

Sometimes you have to change the spelling of the word before
you add the suffix (for example, *fame* ⟶ *famous*).

c   Add –ly or –ous to these words.
Circle the adjectives and underline the adverbs.

5   Spelling rules

Rules about spelling can help you write
words correctly, but remember: there are
some words that don't obey the rules!

Writing tip

Check the spelling of
the words you have
written in a dictionary.

Rules for spelling plural nouns

Add s to most words (for example, *chair* ⟶ *chairs*).

When nouns end in 'hissing' sounds (sh, ch, s, ss, z, zz, x)
add –es (for example, *bus* ⟶ *buses*).

Write the plurals of these nouns in your notebook.

Writing tip

Remember that plural means 'more than one'.

> Term 3 Spelling activities

1 Irregular verbs

We make the past tense of most verbs by adding –ed but some irregular verbs have irregular past tense forms.

Match the verbs in the first box with their past tense forms in the second box. Write the pairs of words in your notebook.

> begin break bring buy catch come do give have hear is make stand think throw

> caught had heard came made broke stood was bought brought thought gave began threw did

2 Prefixes

A prefix is a group of letters added at the beginning of a word. The prefix changes the word's meaning and makes a new word.

a Look at this group of words. What do you think the prefix *re–* means?

repeat   rebuild   return   reappear   renew   refresh

b Look at these words.

invisible   indirect   impossible   illegal   immeasurable
irresponsible   illegible   irrelevant

What do you think the prefix *in–* means?

Match the beginnings and endings of the spelling rules
in the boxes and write the spelling rules in your notebook.

The prefix *in*– becomes *im*– before ...
The prefix *in*– becomes *il*– before ...
The prefix *in*– becomes *ir*– before ...
The prefix *in*– is not changed before ...

words beginning with *m* or *p*.
words beginning with other letters.
words beginning with *r*.
words beginning with *l*.

c The prefix *sub*–means 'under' or 'below', and the word *marine*
   means 'to do with the sea'. So a submarine is a vessel that
   goes under the surface of the sea. Write definitions for these
   words in your notebook. You can look them up in a dictionary.

subway submerge subheading subtract

3 **Homonyms**

Homonyms are words that have more than one meaning.
Complete these pairs of sentences with homonyms.

a People put their money in a ... to keep it safe.

   I like walking along the river ... .

b You ... your hand from side to side when you say goodbye.

   The surfer rode to the shore on a huge ... .

c The shepherd put the sheep in a ... .

   I wrote a letter with my new ... .

d I'm not feeling very ... .

   We collected water from the ... .

e It was an exciting football ... .

   He lit a ... to light a fire.

4 Different letters, same sound

<u>Underline</u> the consonant/s in the words on the right that matches the sounds <u>underlined</u> in the words on the left.

a <u>j</u>ar   giraffe

b <u>wr</u>ite   rain

c nu<u>mb</u>   monkey

d pu<u>dd</u>le   dinosaur

e <u>c</u>ar   kitten deck

5 Spelling strategies

If you don't know how to spell a word, you could:

- use a phoneme frame to divide it up into its sounds
- think of similar word you know how to spell
- think about prefixes and suffixes you already know
- count the syllables and spell each syllable separately
- think about a spelling rule you already know
- shut your eyes and 'see' the word in your head
- think of a calligram for the word
- use a mnemonic.

a Draw calligrams in your notebook for two of these words.

catch over short slow tall

b Write a mnemonic for a word you find hard to remember.

Writing tip

Remember that a **calligram** makes the word into a picture.

Remember that a **mnemonic** is a saying that helps you to remember a spelling.

6 Spelling log

Keep a spelling log to help you learn how to spell difficult words. Look at the spelling mistakes you make in your writing. If you spell a word incorrectly, write it correctly in your log. Identify the bit you found difficult and find other words with the same spelling pattern.

Copy this spelling log into your notebook and fill it in with three words you find tricky to spell.

Word	Tricky bit	Other words with the same spelling pattern		
learn	ear	early	earth	earn

› Toolkit

Different sorts of words

Use these handy reminders to get on top of your grammar!

Nouns	Pronouns	Adjectives
are naming words for people, places and things: *house flowers hope Maria London*	can be used instead of nouns: *I you he she it we they his its mine*	are describing words which tell you more about nouns: *big pretty ordinary terrifying*
Verbs	**Prepositions**	**Connectives**
tell you what someone or something does, is or has: *walk read like write have be take play*	are words that show the relationship between a noun (or pronoun) with another word in the sentence. They often show the 'position' of something. *over by in through*	are joining words that link sentences: *and so but or when although because*

Punctuation

Punctuation adds meaning to a sentence. It helps us to read with expression and understanding.

Full stops	Capital letters	Commas
mark the end of sentences: I love reading.	show the beginning of a sentence, proper nouns and titles: My best friend is Paula.	separate items in a list: I need to buy apples, oranges, bananas and plums.
Exclamation marks	**Question marks**	**Speech marks**
indicate exclamations or commands: Help! There's a dragon!	indicate questions: Where are you going?	show words spoken in dialogue: 'Shall we play a game,' she said.
Apostrophes		
show where two words have been joined together then shortened: The fire isn't burning now. These are also known as contractions.		

Text types

Fiction

Real-life stories

- These are stories about people.
- There is usually more than one character.
- They have real-life settings.
- The main character has a problem.
- Other characters help to solve the problem.
- There is a lot of dialogue to discuss the problem.

Myths and legends

- These are very old stories that were told before they were written down.
- Myths and legends are set a long time ago. They sometimes contain magical elements.
- Many cultures have their own myths and legends, which help to explain the history of the people.
- Myths explain how something began.
- Legends are about heroes and heroines.

Adventure stories

- These are stories in which the main character, or characters, have an adventure.
- They can be real-life stories, stories about invented worlds or stories set in the past.
- The main characters are brave and solve problems.
- The language is exciting with lots of powerful verbs.
- There is often some dialogue.

Non-fiction

Instructions

- These tell you how to do something.
- The opening statement says what the instructions are for.
- There is often a section to tell you what you will need to be able to follow the instructions.
- They are written in order and are often numbered.
- Each instruction begins with a command verb or a sequencing word.
- There is very little descriptive language.

Letters

- These are written for many different reasons.
- The language matches the purpose (for example, friendly, business-like or complaining).
- Most letters begin with *Dear* and end with a finishing comment and a name.
- Postcards contain a short message and often tell about a journey or holiday.

Information texts

- These give information about something.
- The main heading tells you what the information is about.
- Subheadings are used to show you what topic a paragraph or section is about.
- There is usually a contents page. There is often an index.
- The language is factual.
- There are photos, pictures and diagrams to give some of the information.
- There may be captions to tell you what is in a photo.
- There may be labels to explain the different parts of a diagram or picture.

Poetry

Alliteration
A consonant sound that is repeated at the beginning of several words for effect, often found in tongue twisters.
Peter Piper picked a peck of pickled pepper.

Onomatopoeia
Words that sound like their meaning.
zoom   buzz   chirp

Rhyme
Words with the same or similar sounds at the end.

Rhythm
A beat or sound pattern made by syllables when we say words.

Syllable
The unit of sound in words. A syllable is one beat for each part of a word.
ex /   cit /   ing 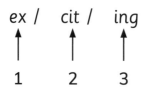   1   2   3

> Key words

⟩ Acknowledgements

The authors and publishers acknowledge the following sources of copyright material and are grateful for the permissions granted. While every effort has been made, it has not always been possible to identify the sources of all the material used, or to trace all copyright holders. If any omissions are brought to our notice, we will be happy to include the appropriate acknowledgements on reprinting.

Unit 1 Excerpt from *Matilda* by Roald Dahl, text copyright 1988 by Roald Dahl. Used by permission of David Higham Associates and Viking Children's Books, an imprint of Penguin Young Readers Group, a division of Penguin Random House LLC. All rights reserved; Excerpt from *Danny The Champion of the World* by Roald Dahl, illustrated by Quentin Blake, copyright 1975 by Roald Dahl. Used by permission of David Higham Associates and Puffin, an imprint of Penguin Young Readers Group, a division of Penguin Random House LLC. All rights reserved; Excerpt from *Charlie and the Chocolate Factory* by Roald Dahl, text copyright 1964 by Roald Dahl. Used by permission of David Higham Associates and Puffin, an imprint of Penguin Young Readers Group, a division of Penguin Random House LLC. All rights reserved; Excerpts from *The Enormous Crocodile* by Roald Dahl, copyright 1978 by Roald Dahl. Used by permission of David Higham Associates and Puffin, an imprint of Penguin Young Readers Group, a division of Penguin Random House LLC. All rights reserved; **Unit 3** 'Dancing Poinciana' by Telecine Turner; 'Hurricane' from *Earth Magic* written by Dionne Brand is used by permission of Kids Can Press Ltd., Toronto. Text Copyright 1979, 2006 Dionne Brand; 'Cat Haiku' by Kobayashi Issa; *Coral Reef* written by Clare Bevan is used by the permission of the author; **Unit 4** 'Bear and Fire' S.E Schlosser and AmericanFolklore.net. Copyright 2014. All rights reserved; Extracts from *Sinbad and the Roc* by Ian Whybrow, illustrated by Nick Schon, Cambridge Reading Adventures, Cambridge University Press, used by kind permission of the author; **Unit 6** Extract from *Four Clever Brothers* by Lynne Rickards, illustrated by Galia Bernstein © Cambridge University Press and UCL Institute of Education, 2017; **Unit 7** Extract and illustrations from *Alfie Small: Pirates and Dragons* and *Alfie Small: Ug and the Dinosaurs* by Nick Ward, copyright copyright by Nick Ward 2010, published by David Fickling Books 2012. Reprinted by permission of Penguin Books Limited; Extract from *Who's a Clever Girl, Then?* by Rose Impey, published by Egmont; Extracts from *Dragon Boy* by Pippa Goodhart, illustrated by Martin Ursell, Reprinted by permission of HarperCollins Publishers Ltd, copyright 2003 Pippa Goodhart and Martin Ursell; **Unit 8** *Caribbean Islands* by Alice Harman, Wayland. Reproduced by permission of Wayland, an imprint of Hachette Children's Books; **Unit 9** 'Wordspinning' by John Foster from *The Works*, reproduced by permission of author; 'Starter' from *Smile, Please* by Tony Bradman. Reproduced by permission of The Agency (London) Ltd. Copyright Tony Bradman, 1986, First published by Viking; 'Kite' by June Crebbin, originally in *The Crocodile is Coming*, June Crebbin, Walker Books 2005.

Thanks to the following for permission to reproduce images:

Cover image by Pablo Gallego (Beehive Illustration); *Inside* **Unit 1** Rich Legg/GI; Toxawww/GI; Jordan Siemens/GI; FooTToo/GI; Leonard McCombe/GI; Konoplytska/GI; Amveale/GI; Vibrant Pictures/Alamy Stock Photo; Songsak Wilairit /GI; Graham Dowd/GI; USO/GI; DianaLynne/GI; Lew Robertson, Brand X Pictures/GI; Jose Luis Pelaez Inc/GI; Sean_Warren/GI; **Unit 2** NurPhoto/GI; Kali9/GI; Carl De Souza/GI; simonlong/GI; albkdb/GI; kali9/GI; TeresaKasprzycka/GI; Kali9/GI; Portland Press Herald/GI; XiXinXing/GI; Betsie Van der Meer/GI; **Unit 3** Juanmonino/GI; AFP Contributor/GI; Blend Images - REB Images/GI; Arnab Bora/GI; Manoj Shah/GI; Turmite/GI; Bullyphoto/GI; Katrin Sauerwein/GI; StuPorts/GI; Jacky Parker Photography/GI; Brian Mckay Photographyy/GI; Georgette Douwma/GI; **Unit 4** Ryan McVay/GI; Marco Pozzi Photographer/GI; Vyacheslav Argenberg/GI; Walter Bibikow/GI; Mtcurado/GI; Hindustan Times/GI; John Seaton Callahan/GI; Hindustan Times/GI; **Unit 5** Susie Adams/GI; Patrick Pleul/GI; The India Today Group/GI; Matt Cardy/GI; Alison Wright/GI; Maica/GI; Images By Tang Ming Tung/GI; Arvind Balaraman/GI; JGI/Jamie Grill/GI; Martin Barraud/GI; Kirill Rudenko/GI; Seb Oliver/GI; Christian C/GI; kali9/GI; Martin Barraud/GI; **Unit 6** Jupiterimages/GI; Marji Lang/GI; Carol Yepes/GI; Hill Street Studios/GI; **Unit 7** Image Source/GI; Wavebreakmedia/GI; fstop123/GI; Design Pics/GI; John Lund/GI; Epoxydude/GI; Prasngkh Ta Kha/EyeEm/GI; PBNJ Productions/GI; **Unit 8** SeanPavonePhoto/GI; Leisa Tyler/GI; GeorgePeters/GI; Val Thoermer/GI; Peter Cade/GI; Karen Desjardin/GI; cinoby/GI; nantonov/GI; Flavio Vallenari/GI; Roberto Moiola/Sysaworld/GI; Mike Hill/GI; Bloomberg Creative/GI; levente bodo/GI; Andrew Peacock/GI; Marc Guitard/GI; John W Banagan/GI; simonbradfield/GI; Omersukrugoksu/GI; John White Photos/GI; FiledIMAGE/GI; Victor Rubow / GI; Natasha Maiolo/GI; Ted Mead/GI; Drazen/GI; Marco Bottigelli/GI; Tim Hall/GI; JGI/Jamie Grill/GI; FatCamera/GI; **Unit 9** Noor Iskandar/GI; FatCamera/GI; **Unit 10** Peter Dazeley/GI; Chonticha Vatpongpee/GI; Todd Ryburn/GI; Vi Vien Lee/GI; Gonzalo Azumendi/GI; Roger Harris/SPL/GI; Zentilia/GI

Key: GI= Getty Images